I'd Rather Be Working

I'd Rather Be Working

A Step-by-Step Guide to
Financial Self-Support for People
with Chronic Illness

GAYLE BACKSTROM

AMACOM

American Management Association
New York • Atlanta • Brussels • Buenos Aires • Chicago • London • Mexico City
San Francisco • Shanghai • Tokyo • Toronto • Washington, D.C.

*Special discounts on bulk quantities of AMACOM books are
available to corporations, professional associations, and
other organizations. For details, contact Special Sales
Department, AMACOM, a division of American Management
Association, 1601 Broadway, New York, NY 10019.
Tel.: 212-903-8316. Fax: 212-903-8083.
Web site: www.amacombooks.org*

*This publication is designed to provide accurate and
authoritative information in regard to the subject matter covered.
It is sold with the understanding that the publisher is not engaged
in rendering medical, legal, accounting, or other professional
service. If legal advice or other expert assistance is required, the
services of a competent professional person should be sought.*

Library of Congress Cataloging-in-Publication Data

Backstrom, Gayle.
    *I'd rather be working : a step-by-step guide to financial self-support
for people with chronic illness / Gayle Backstrom.*
        p.   cm.
    Includes bibliographical references and index.
    ISBN 0-8144-7115-3
    1. Chronically ill—Finance, Personal.   I. Title.
RA644.5 .B335 2002
362.1'96044—dc21   *2002003939*

Printing number

10   9   8   7   6   5   4   3   2   1

To Maurine Burnett, who has been there for me so many times, providing support and encouragement, especially during the writing of this book. By taking care of the everyday chores, she has made it possible for me to focus on my writing.

Maurine, this one is for you.

Contents

Foreword

The National Organization on Disability maintains that the case for employing people with disabilities in the United States has never been stronger. Despite downturns in the economy, it is important to consider this in context, and people with disabilities seeking employment should remain positive about their opportunities for employment. The need for skilled labor continues in the United States, and the need for people with disabilities to play a key role in meeting the labor needs was reinforced by Thomas J. Donohue, U.S. Chamber of Commerce president and CEO, at the National Workplace Forum held on September 10, 2001.

There are four key trends converging that call for compelling action to add more people with disabilities to the nation's workforce: economic growth, which runs in cycles but is still expected to pick up after the recession of 2001; a short supply of labor; an aging workforce; and a growing, savvy recognition of the strong consumer market of people with disabilities. Already comprising one of five people in the United States, people with disabilities represent a spending powerhouse: a projected one trillion dollars in 2001 in annual aggregate consumer spending, according to a 1997 report from the marketing research firm Packaged Facts. Other research shows that households with one or more persons with disabilities are significantly more likely to do business with disability-friendly companies, and that consumers (with and without disabilities) are more likely to purchase goods and services from companies that address disability issues.

Furthermore, people with disabilities themselves must remain aware that the impact their peers with disabilities have had on the workplace has been an extremely positive one, and has created an advantage that corporate leaders and CEOs will not give up. To that end, Gayle Backstrom, in *I'd Rather Be Working*, provides a much-needed resource for people whose chronic illness affects their ability to work, and who want to reap the financial and other rewards that employment affords.

—Craig Gray, Director of EmployAbility
National Organization on Disability, September 14, 2001

Preface

What This Book Will Do for You

If you (or someone close to you) are one of the millions of people whose ability to work and support themselves and their dependents has been compromised by chronic illness, *I'd Rather Be Working* provides a practical hands-on guide to help you evaluate your present situation (especially regarding employability), seek out education and training, and find a job or career that best utilizes your skills and abilities.

I'd Rather Be Working is a guide to circumventing the limitations of chronic illness. It will help you evaluate your experience and interests, and determine the kind of work you can do and would be happy doing. The goal is to help you find work that will enable you to support yourself, or at least contribute to that support. This guide can be used no matter the severity of your chronic illness. For some of you, it may be important to change jobs to prevent your chronic illness from becoming worse.

One in five Americans has a disability, so you and I are clearly not alone in our struggle to survive both chronic illness and financial hardship. Many men and women have created careers for themselves in spite of their illnesses. In this book, I share not only my experiences, but also those of other individuals who have changed the way they work because of their chronic illness.

I'd Rather Be Working includes individual examples, self-evaluation exercises, quizzes, lists, and extensive resource lists. It shows you how to take advantage of today's rapidly changing marketplace so you may match your knowledge and experience, as well as your limitations, to current or expected needs, and find ways to earn money as well as achieve personal satisfaction. In addition, it:

- Addresses the Ticket to Work program as well as other government programs that provide services and advantages that can be vital to disabled persons who are drawing disability income

- Discusses the concept of "reasonable accommodation" and gives examples of common accommodations

- Helps you evaluate and research the markets for your goods and services, if you choose self-employment

- Shows you how to avoid the increasing numbers of tempting "money-for-nothing" scams

- Shows you how to harness the infinite resources of the Internet in locating opportunities

- Provides information from experts on career guidance, work accommodations, personal assessment, and vocational rehabilitation

- Includes further resources for you to pursue on your own

- Provides much-needed moral support if you have despaired of ever working again

This book will provide a blueprint that will enable you to determine just how your past work experience, skills, knowledge, personal interests, and personality traits can assist you in looking for a full- or part-time job that offers enough flexibility to accommodate your illness. It will also help you evaluate whether you should build your own business, custom-made to fit your abilities and your limitations. It is not necessarily simple, quick, or easy, but it is a workable program.

The old adage of a successful business—"Find a need and fill it"—still applies. Although it was originally used for building a new business through self-employment, it also can be applied to evaluating existing employment positions. The adage just needs to be adapted to accommodate one's illness. *I'd Rather Be Working* shows you how to do just that and leads you through the necessary steps to achieve financial security.

The book has two primary focuses: how to continue working as an employee (by means of various adaptations and accommodations), and how to evaluate the possibility of becoming self-employed by beginning a small business. Another factor in your search for employment will be the changing ways in which work is being done today, such as telecommuting and home businesses.

The exercises and suggestions in this book can be used by anyone with any form of chronic illness, as they are not disease specific. While the primary audience is individuals with chronic illnesses, the book can also be used by health-care professionals and advocates, vocational rehabilitation trainers, and employers.

Acknowledgments

Many people have been instrumental in getting this book written and I want to express my appreciation to them. My agent, Jim Donovan, and his assistant, Kathryn Lindsey, worked very hard with me on developing the proposal and submitting the manuscript for publication. Ellen Kadin, my editor at AMACOM; Dianne Estridge, her assistant; Christina McLaughlin, development editor; Erika Spelman, associate editor, who took the book through the production process; Kama Timbrell, publicity; and Vera Sarkanj, special sales, were all a tremendous help in working on the book to make it a stronger publication. Thanks to Erin Hunter for proofing the manuscript, especially on such short notice. I also want to thank Susan Hunter for her work as copy editor.

Working on a book such as this involves a lot of research and I want to thank Dr. Julia Newcomer, assistant professor of management, School of Management, Texas Woman's University, Denton, Texas, for her assistance in this area. I want to thank the individuals who responded to my request for input on their experiences in working with a chronic illness.

Thanks also to Craig Gray, Director of EmployAbility, National Organization on Disability, for providing the foreword, giving encouragement for individuals with disabilities even in light of the current economic trends.

I also need to thank my fellow writers, Donna Bell and Billie Cantwell, who supported, listened, encouraged, and kept me on track even when I thought my health problems would keep me from finishing the book. I couldn't have done it without you.

The writers of the Kiss of Death Chapter of Romance Writers of America online group, Clues-N-News, also encouraged me when the going got rough.

No acknowledgment could be complete without including the members of my health-care team, Dr. Bernard Rubin, rheumatologist, and Dr. Elizabeth John, psychiatrist, who have helped me understand and cope with my fibromyalgia and the complications of living with it.

—Gayle Backstrom

Introduction

Sandra was in her twenties and training to be a teacher when rheumatoid arthritis changed her world. For several years she received Social Security disability payments until, as she puts it, "I decided that the people of this country hadn't given me arthritis, so why should I make them pay for it." She wrote novels for several years without success, but when a neighbor predicted that she would never be published, Sandra set out to prove her wrong. She has subsequently published more than twenty novels to date and is the recipient of several awards for her books. She was one of the very first romance writers to dare write about a heroine who had an incurable illness— rheumatoid arthritis.

Sandra and I are only two of many in the United States today who must strive to overcome the limitations of a chronic illness (CI) to become or to remain self-supporting. To a person newly diagnosed with a chronic disease, the task of reordering one's life and career can seem impossible.

For others, the course of their CI has progressed to the point where it is now interfering with their ability to keep their present job or to work at all. I don't know how many times I have heard or read of people with fibromyalgia (FM) or chronic fatigue syndrome saying that they must keep working if they are to survive financially. But the only way they have the energy to work is by spending much of their time outside of work in bed.

In 1986, when I told an internist at Scott and White Medical Clinic, in Temple, Texas, that that was how I was living, he told me "That's not living. It's existing." It may be "just existing," but if you have no other source of income, you still have to keep plugging away to support yourself and often a family as well. The situation could be the same with any number of other chronic illnesses.

I have found that by carefully and honestly examining one's skills

1

and physical limitations, it is often possible to create a fulfilling and financially satisfying career. If the limitations imposed by your CI are severe enough, you may have to lower your expectations, but you may still bring in some money and feel a sense of accomplishment in what you are doing.

The goal is to find a way to minimize the limitations, work around them, and at the same time maximize the income potential. It takes me a lot longer to write now than it did before my illness affected my abilities; it's difficult and painful. But while FM and other health problems keep me from doing as much as I would like, I still write. I have switched to using a speech recognition program because pain in my hands has become severe, and this new technology has helped me finish this book. This is just an example of how you can use the process in this book to achieve your goals.

There are other individuals whose chronic illness does not keep them from working, but it does make some parts of their job more difficult. Many times there are ways to change the way you perform a job that eases that difficulty. This is accommodation.

The fact remains that each individual's situation is unique. Some people will be able to work with only minor changes to their usual process, while others must make changes as drastic as those I have made. I want to emphasize this: Every individual is different, her situation is different, and this must be taken into consideration when looking at the exercises in this book and her future.

When a Door Closes, Open the Window

Several times over the last twenty years I have found myself in situations where I had to do some creative job searching. When the oil bust hit Wichita Falls, Texas, in 1980 and the region's economy was affected, I was forced to close my public relations firm. During the next few years I faced difficult times; my FM flared up and I worked at a number of part-time jobs, getting occasional income from activities such as direct sales of cosmetics and jewelry, portrait photography, and office temp work. In 1987, I had to give up my full-time employment as a high-school librarian and teacher and work at whatever part-time jobs I was able to perform, such as college adjunct instructor. Even that became difficult as my chronic pain and fatigue grew. Finally, in 1994, the Veterans Administration agreed that my fibromyalgia and its accompanying conditions were 100 percent disabling, and I now have a disability check to live on.

But, as many individuals who receive a disability check, whether from a private insurance program, Social Security, or the Veterans Administration, can tell you, a disability check is not always *enough* to live on. In fact, the Social Security Administration states that the disability benefits it pays usually are not enough to raise the disabled individual and his family above poverty level. While not everyone with a disability is living in poverty, a high percentage of those who do live at poverty level have some form of disability or health limitations. Their primary concern must always be provision for the basic necessities of life: food, clothing, and shelter.

At times, and with increasing frequency as my CI worsened, my physical inability to work full-time or at occupations that required a lot of energy prevented me from getting any income beyond my disability check. So, how did I manage? I had to reevaluate my work skills, interests, and the work options available to me, and I made the most of opportunities and alternative work skills. Very seldom did I find a job in the classified ads.

Why We Work

Money is certainly the primary motive for anyone to work, but there is another reason that is almost as important: the need for accomplishment, the need to be productive and to contribute something to the world around you.

Over the years, there have been numerous theories on why individuals work and how they are motivated. Abraham Maslow, a psychologist and philosopher, developed a "hierarchy of needs" theory that establishes higher-order and lower-order needs.[1] The lower-order needs include physiological, safety, and social needs. Maslow believes that man must first provide the most basic of human needs: food, clothing, shelter, and sex, then ensure security, protection, and stability of daily life. The next step was to meet the need for love, affection, and a sense of belonging in regard to other individuals.

Once those basic life necessities have been met, however, Maslow believes that individuals then seek to meet such needs as self-esteem, respect from others, and a personal sense of competency before moving on to the highest level, where he believes individuals grow and use their abilities to the fullest.

Unless someone has been faced with the difficulties of providing the basics of living, it is hard for that person to understand just how completely they can dominate a person's life. It's also difficult for someone to realize just how much our identity is wrapped up in what we do for a living until she can no longer perform that role.

Like it or not, our society usually views us in terms of whether we work or not, and what type of work we do. Most opening conversations between strangers include questions about work and jobs. Even between acquaintances and friends, where we work and how our jobs are going is a primary topic of discussion. When our ability to get or keep a job is compromised, we feel a strong sense of loss—of worth, of independence, of control—and often a loss of identity. That's why, when given a choice, most people would prefer working.

Studies have shown that only 29 percent of disabled persons of working age (18–64) work full- or part-time compared with 79 percent of the nondisabled population. But, when surveyed by the National Organization on Disability in 1998, 72 percent of those with disabilities who were of working age and who were not currently employed stated they'd "rather be working."[2]

For many of those with CIs or disabilities who would rather be working, quite often some sort of "accommodation" can be made that will enable them to work. For me, the voice recognition software was less than $200 and the light keyboard was $200. That is less than the average amount of $500 needed for the majority of accommodations that can make the difference between working and not working. Quite often, common sense alone, when applied to the situation, will provide the accommodation without any added costs.

Self-Management of Your Chronic Illness Is a Must

Chronic illnesses are defined by the Centers for Disease Control as those illnesses that are prolonged, do not resolve spontaneously, and are rarely cured completely. CIs account for the majority of those with disabilities. The impact of chronic illnesses varies from individual to individual, with some having only minor problems in performing daily activities, whether personal, work, or recreational. There are others, though, whose illnesses have placed a major burden upon them, affecting their abilities to carry out their normal daily activities. To some degree, these individuals are now facing a disability.

I believe that it is possible to live a full and satisfying life in spite of and with a CI. Your frame of mind will often determine how well you are able to cope with your illness. Your attitude toward your illness, your limitations, your skills and abilities, and your prospects for employment in whatever capacity you can attain could very well make the difference between success or failure. Does that put all of the blame on your shoulders if you don't find employment? If your symptoms remain out of control, keeping you from retraining or working, is that your fault?

No. You must first make the decision that you are going to do everything you can to self-manage your CI. You are going to take care of yourself the way you would take care of someone you loved who had such an illness. It's been said that we are often far harder on ourselves than we would be on anyone else. So, start by loving yourself. That means accepting your illness, your limitations, even the altered body image many of us develop when illness strikes. Don't sit down in a chair or crawl into bed and pull the covers over your head. You are entitled to some "down" time, but you must focus on using your energies and skills to the best of your present ability.

By self-management, I mean that you must take the medication prescribed by your doctor, and follow any recommendations she has made for nutrition and exercise. You must educate yourself regarding your illness, then learn to listen to your body. I'll go into more detail in Chapter 1.

Attitude

I would like to make a note here about attitude. For years, I didn't think of myself as disabled. "Disabled" meant someone who was paralyzed because of a spinal cord injury or was hearing or visually impaired. I had "health problems." Yes, I had to restrict my working activities and my daily living activities. And, yes, I began to use a cane in 1988, a wheelchair in 1989, and then an electric scooter in 1990. It was true that I could not get or keep a job and finally received my disability compensation from the Veterans Administration in 1994. But, I had "health problems"; I wasn't "disabled."

It really wasn't until August 2000, when I developed peripheral neuropathy and could no longer walk around my house without severe pain, that I began to reluctantly change my mind. In May 2001,

I switched to an electric wheelchair. The first time I sat down in that wheelchair, I swore I heard the word *disabled* screamed out.

Neither my friends nor my psychiatrist could see any difference in the means of mobility for me or understand why I went into a depression once I got the new chair. But it was my attitude that made the difference. Intellectually, I had known all along that my health problems were disabling, but I didn't want to think of myself that way. My electric scooter was just an easier way to get around. It didn't "feel" disabled.

I bring this up because throughout this book, I will be talking about different levels of limitations caused by chronic illnesses. I do not want to put anyone off because they do not feel they are "disabled" or have a "disabling condition." I want this book to be a positive experience. I want readers to get whatever they need from this book to help them reach whatever goals they may have, whether it is to meet basic living needs or to find financial security by working around their health problems. Just as everyone's health conditions and limitations are different, so are their goals. I want to help you find your way, despite your limitations, whether they are minor or disabling.

So, remember that attitude has a great deal to do with how you face your personal reality. Don't let that attitude keep you from taking advantage of whatever help is available for you, whether it is a technological aid such as voice recognition software or a more involved "accommodation" that you are entitled to because of the Americans with Disabilities Act (ADA).

Whether you need to change the way you currently do one activity in your present job, completely change your career, or switch to a part-time occupation, I hope you will find this book helpful. And if you are one of those people whose CI keeps you from working even part-time, I believe there is still something for you in this book that will lead you to some activity that will give you a sense of accomplishment at whatever level you are able to handle.

Quality of Life

When an individual without a disability looks for employment, she must determine how much time she will spend on leisure activities and how much time will be spent working. For individuals with disabilities and specifically CIs, there may be far less leisure time available to them. Just basic living activities take much longer and require more energy expenditures than for those without disabilities. It doesn't matter whether the extra energy needs to be utilized in personal care or in housework; there is still less energy available for work. When an individual with a disability begins to look for employment, he must take into consideration all of the demands upon his energy. When an individual with a disability must choose between work and leisure activities, he must think about the overall quality of life he will have and how much work he can and chooses to do.

The Job Market for Workers with Chronic Illness

What happens to those with CIs or disabilities when the overall economy is in a downturn or recession, and the individual has no control over his employment? During 1999 and early in the year 2000, the overall economic picture in the United States was at an all-time high, yet those with chronic illnesses and disabilities were not sharing in the prosperity.

An estimated 1.2 million Americans lost their jobs from January through August 2001, a reflection that the economy was in trouble. By late November 2001, the United States was officially declared to be in a recession that had actually begun somewhere around March 2001.

Historically, the economy operates in a cyclical pattern and even though no one at this writing is predicting just when it will improve this time, that fact should not be used as an excuse to continue to deny individuals with CIs the opportunity to work. The terrorist attacks on September 11, 2001, also had a very strong effect on the economy, with thousands of people losing their jobs.

It is still too early to tell how the weakened economy and rising unemployment will directly affect those individuals with disabilities, but they may encounter many of the same problems of older workers who have been laid off. Traditionally, it has been very difficult for workers over fifty to find new employment if they have been let go. Despite the slowing economy, predictions are that there are jobs available. Some experts are expecting full employment by 2025.

This book is not intended to be a substitute for proper medical care by a physician, nor proper legal advice regarding disability rights, whether under the ADA or any other federal, state, or other law or regulation. It is intended to be a guide. It does not offer an easy solution for the individual, but, if used properly, it can provide an important reference tool. In short, this is a guide to help you achieve your goals, and it all starts with a self-evaluation. So let's get started.

Notes

1. Abraham Maslow, *Motivation and Personality,* 2nd ed. (New York: Harper Collins, 1970).

2. National Organization on Disability, 1998 N.O.D./Harris Survey of Americans with Disabilities.

PART I

Self-Evaluation

CHAPTER One

Where Am I and
Where Am I Going?

Because each chronic illness (CI) and its impact upon the individual varies, each person must take a clear, realistic account of his own situation. Two people of the same age and sex will have a different experience with the same diagnosis, even though they may have many of the same symptoms. Since the purpose of this book is to help you keep your current job, or find different work that you can do within your physical limitations (either in your present company or in an existing position somewhere else), or become self-employed, you must examine your present situation.

I recommend that you use a three-ring binder to hold the materials that you will produce in working through this book. If you use a computer to record your thoughts and responses, save the information on a disk or on your hard drive, but I also suggest that you print out the information and place it in the binder. The physical act of writing down this information often helps you recall things you might not have remembered otherwise, and with it printed out and saved in the binder, you can refer to it at any time. The physical presence of the words on a page will also make the project more real to you.

Goals and plans for meeting them are discussed in Chapter 3, but this first chapter's work gives you a clear picture of where you stand, physically, mentally, financially, and socially, as well as helps you determine whether you have a physical and emotional support system.

Your Diagnosis, Your Doctor, and Your Medical Team

The first place to start is with the actual diagnosis of your CI. Although it would be very nice to say that a person will only have one

11

chronic illness at a time and that he will receive an immediate and definite diagnosis, it isn't very realistic. Sometimes it may take months or even years to receive a definitive diagnosis, particularly for some illnesses that do not have a specific medical test that can say, "Yes, you have this disease." For certain illnesses, doctors must first rule out other illnesses and then make a diagnosis by taking a complete medical history and considering your symptoms.

Certain health conditions may occur *because* of the CI, and some health conditions may commonly *accompany* an illness. And sometimes, certain conditions just happen to a person regardless of any other health problems. It is not uncommon for people with either rheumatoid arthritis or systemic lupus also to have fibromyalgia (FM). Those with diabetes often develop problems with their eyes, kidneys, or heart, as well as with the nerves or blood circulation in their feet. Depression often accompanies many CIs and may be a result of the emotional problems of coping with that chronic illness or an unrelated condition.

As an example, FM is often accompanied by one or more of the following secondary conditions: irritable bowel syndrome; migraine or tension-type headaches; multiple chemical sensitivities to foods, drugs, or scents; depression; chronic fatigue syndrome (CFS); regional myofascial pain syndrome; temporomandibular pain and dysfunction syndrome in the jaw; restless leg syndrome; periodic limb movement; and primary dysmenorrhea (painful menstruation). Not everyone with FM has all or even many of these conditions and the severity of the symptoms varies. Many of these conditions are not, in themselves, disabling, but the combination of them with a more serious CI can put limitations on the individual that make it difficult to work.

What is your particular CI, and is it physical or mental? Usually, knowing the nature of your CI is fairly straightforward. When your doctor has given you a particular diagnosis, learning about that illness is an important step in learning to live with it. Today's patient should be an active participant in her health care and become educated about the disease. In past years, the patient was a passive participant in health care, but today's patients are generally actively working to take care of themselves under the guidance of health-care professionals.

Do you have a medical team for your health care? For example, for someone with rheumatoid arthritis, the team could consist of a rheumatologist, a psychiatrist or perhaps a psychologist, and a physical or occupational therapist. With today's managed health care, you will probably have a primary care physician to coordinate your health care. It also helps to have all of your medications filled at one pharmacy. If different doctors prescribe different medications, the pharmacist will be able to watch for any potential drug interactions. Whatever health-care professionals you have on your team, it is ultimately your responsibility to be informed about your CI.

Your Limitations

Today many doctors can provide copies of clinical and laboratory findings, but some find it difficult to say that a person can or cannot perform all of the required duties of a particular job. This is often because they don't know exactly what specific physical or mental activities are involved in performing your job, not because they don't know what the impact of the disease is upon the body.

The doctor may be able to tell you that you should not lift more than X number of pounds, walk more than X number of feet, and so on. You are the one who knows whether you have to lift objects or walk distances in your job. So it will be up to the two of you to work together on determining the limitations on your physical and mental work-related functions. For example, if fatigue is a major problem with your chronic illness, you may find it difficult to work a regular eight-hour workday, and you will do better with a more flexible schedule. You might need to come in later and then work later to put in the necessary hours to complete your work. Or you might be able to telecommute for several days during the week. If you have problems walking, but not sitting, and your job requires you to be on your feet a lot, that is important to note.

Physical

Do you have problems with any of the following physical activities? List only those that limit your activities in either personal or your work environment.

Sitting

- Does prolonged sitting, such as at a desk and computer or in a vehicle, cause pain or fatigue?

■ Can you sit down and/or get out of a regular chair without assistance?

Standing

■ How long can you stand?

■ Do you have a problem with maintaining your balance, either when standing or walking?

■ Can you stand without any support, or do you need assistance such as leaning on a piece of furniture or using a cane, walker, etc.?

Walking

■ How far can you walk without pain or fatigue?

■ Do you use some form of assistance to walk, such as a cane, crutches, or a walker?

■ Do you need a wheelchair or electric scooter to get around, for in-house use, outside your own home, shopping, working, or leisure activities?

Movement

■ Can you raise your arms above your head, to get an item down off a shelf or reach some part of a machine? What about reaching out in front of you or to either side?

■ Can you lift an object with your extended arm and bring it back to your body? (This isn't good ergonomics even if you don't have anything wrong with you.)

■ How heavy an object can you lift and carry?

■ Can you lift an object from the floor and place it on a table or shelf at your waist height, properly using the muscles in your thighs rather than bending over from the waist?

■ Can you lift an object from the floor and then carry it five feet, ten feet, or farther?

Dexterity

■ Can you use all of your fingers to pick up an object, to operate a piece of equipment, to type on a computer keyboard, or to use a calculator?

■ Do repeated activities cause you pain (e.g., the motions involved in using a computer keyboard, cash register, calculator, or tools such as screwdrivers, hammers, wrenches)?

Overall Physical Activity

■ Have you had to restrict your physical activities because of your chronic illness?

■ What about changes in your personal care routines, such as giving up the use of makeup because it takes too much time and energy to put it on? Have you gotten a different hairstyle that is easier to care for, one that doesn't require you to use blow dryers, curling irons, or such?

■ Have you stopped doing routine house chores, because you lack the energy or they cause you pain?

■ Have you stopped running daily errands for personal business?

■ Have you given up leisure activities in which you had previously participated, or have you stopped taking part in religious or social activities?

■ Have you had to stop working, change jobs, or cut down the number of hours you formerly worked because of your chronic illness?

Mental

Ask yourself the following questions to determine the mental effects of your CI:

■ Have you been diagnosed with a mental health illness such as depression or bipolar disorder? Do you have ongoing medical care for this illness? Are you on any medications for it? (It is very common for individuals with a chronic illness to have problems with depression. This is one reason to have a good mental health specialist as a part of your medical team.)

■ Have you lost interest in activities you previously enjoyed?

■ Has there been a change in the sexual relationship with your spouse or significant other?

- Do you find it hard to motivate yourself?

- Do you have problems concentrating? Are you easily distracted? Do you forget what you were going to say, what you walked into another room to get?

- Do you have a hard time learning new information, such as in a college class, training program, or new duties in your job?

- Do you forget how to do something you have done in the past? (I'm not talking about something like Alzheimer's disease, which many of us automatically fear, if we find ourselves becoming forgetful. That is much more serious than what I'm looking for here.)

- Do you find yourself not being able to come up with the right word, either in conversation or in writing? (That has happened to me so many times in writing this book.)

The physical symptoms of many illnesses can also have an impact on your ability to handle mental work-related functions. Many jobs entail operating equipment, whether it is a computer or manufacturing machinery. Chronic pain or fatigue can make it difficult to concentrate. Some conditions also tend to cause problems with short-term memory.

Individuals with FM and CFS often have problems with cognitive functions, and until fairly recently those problems were met with skepticism. However, special brain scans have shown that the areas of the brain that deal with these cognitive functions often have an insufficient blood flow, which can cause problems.

Also, it is not unusual for medications to affect the way we concentrate and they may also impair judgment and coordination. Most such medications will usually carry warnings regarding driving a vehicle or operating machinery, but there are no guarantees on how a particular medicine will affect a particular person. It is usually a good idea to take precautions when beginning a new medication until you know how it affects you.

Besides the use of equipment, typical mental work-related functions include understanding, remembering, and following instructions; using appropriate judgment; and responding appropriately to supervision, coworkers, and usual work situations, including changes in a routine work setting.

Emotional

You will need to take a good look at your emotional state, which is separate from your mental state. For years Western medicine has tried to separate the mind and body when treating a patient. But recent research and increased awareness of the link between the mind and body have shown us that everything is linked.

When I write about the mental and emotional aspects of your health, it is definitely *not* an attempt to say that everything is in your head. So many individuals who have illnesses that are hard to diagnose have been told that their symptoms are all in their head or it's just psychological. One woman who responded to my questionnaire wrote that when she saw her doctor about her symptoms, he told her she was afraid of failing, so she would work and put herself into a position where she could fail. When she told him she had just sold a book to a major publisher, he turned around without hesitation and said that she was afraid of success. This is the kind of help we can do without. When I hear of this type of attitude, I would like to give the doctor an "attitude adjustment," nonviolently of course, but still rather strongly. I wonder whether the doctors who make such statements ever actually listen to what they are saying.

Emotions are a part of how we respond to our CI and to its impact on our lives, so it is important that you take a look at how you are handling your emotions. Ask yourself these questions:

- Have you gone through the grief stages regarding your health? (See Appendix A for a good book on the stages of grief.)

- Are you full of anger regarding your chronic illness and your present life (not all anger is bad—sometimes it is necessary to get us moving)?

- Have you come to terms with your chronic illness?

- Are you in denial regarding your chronic illness?

- Do you take your feelings of anger and frustration out on those around you?

- Do you use your chronic illness as a way to manipulate those around you to make them do what you want them to do?

Self-Esteem

How is your self-esteem? How do you feel about yourself? Does your internal voice constantly put you down, especially when you are unable to do something you had been doing before your CI showed up?

Nathaniel Branden, Ph.D., who has been called the father of the self-esteem movement, defines self-esteem as "confidence in our ability to think and to cope with the challenges of life, and confidence in our right to be happy, the feeling of being worthy, deserving, entitled to assert our needs and wants and to enjoy the fruits of our efforts."[1]

The entire issue of self-esteem has been examined in great detail over the last twenty years, and yet some of us still don't realize the importance of having a strong sense of self-esteem. It is in understanding how we value ourselves that we learn how to cope with life and everything that it sends our way. It eases our understanding of others around us.

Although some psychologists have stated that our sense of self-worth is determined by how our parents treated us as children, in fact it is a great deal more complicated than that. It is very easy to blame all of your problems on the fact that you grew up in a "dysfunctional family," and yet it is hard to find a family that isn't dysfunctional in some way or another. Ideally, parents should nurture their children's psyche as well as their body and mind, but when they don't manage to do a very good job of it, we generally do survive. Without getting into the "nurture versus nature" argument about which has the greater influence on us, we can find many individuals who have a healthy sense of self-worth, despite difficult childhoods.

What about self-esteem and CI and how the two are linked to working? The starting point is how we think about our body image. Despite some progress in recognizing that it's okay not to wear a size six dress or have broad shoulders and a lean stomach, when it comes to physical changes caused by illness or accidents, our self-esteem and self-confidence often take a major blow.

Branden states the following about the importance of self-esteem: "The higher our self-esteem, the better equipped we are to cope with life's adversities; the more resilient we are, the more we resist pressure to succumb to despair or defeat."[2] Coping with a CI involves us mentally, emotionally, and spiritually, while dragging us down physically. This book is not intended as a place to deal with issues of self-esteem, other than to let you know that your sense of self-esteem is linked with your self-confidence. Your levels of self-esteem and self-confidence both play a strong part in your ability to accept your chronic illness and its impact on you physically, as well as to deal with its impact on your ability to work.

Branden insists that it is not necessary to like that impact, but you must accept that impact as part of you. By accepting the CI and its impact, you can then move forward in your life. Some people cannot get beyond the fact that they can no longer do the physical activities they were accustomed to before chronic illness hit. That inability will hamper your efforts to find or create work, so you must deal with it.

In my case, there are times when I really don't like the way my body looks now, but I do accept it. If I am not really happy with my physical body, I am content with my mental and emotional states. I know who I am and I am proud of what I have accomplished and how I have dealt with adversities. I have learned that humor and faith make it possible to live with almost anything. I also must say that the road to this point has not always been an easy one.

Once you have drawn a complete and honest picture of the physical, mental, and emotional limitations caused by your health, it is time to look at the other aspects of your life.

Your World

The following exercises are designed to help you get a clear picture of your present resources and circumstances. The idea is that once you know exactly where you stand in these areas, you will have a better idea of what it will take for you to meet the goals you will work on in Chapter 3. In Chapter 2, we explore your education and your experience, but those exercises take you much further than the typical resume does.

The following questions will help you obtain a clear picture of your world, including your financial status, your physical situation, the availability of health care insurance for you and your family, your social life, and what type of support system you have both emotionally and physically.

Financial Status

Answer the following questions first:

- Are you employed (full-time, part-time, or self-employed)?

- Do you receive payments from temporary private disability insurance, Social Security disability, workers' compensation, Veteran's

Administration service-connected disability, or Social Security retirement?

- Are you the sole support of your household? Do you live alone or with a spouse and/or family members? Do you rent or own your own home?

No one but you will ever see the answers that you give in these exercises, so I want you to be completely honest. It is surprising how many individuals really don't know just how they stand financially. They think they are doing fine, but they may really be living from paycheck to paycheck with high levels of credit card debt. Or they may feel they are on shaky ground, only to sit down and look at their overall finances and find they have a healthy cushion that might help them take the time to go to college for a degree, or go back for a new one. They might even be in a position to start their own business.

I am not making any judgments or assumptions in suggesting this exercise. There are individuals and families who know almost to the penny how much they owe and how much they own. And there are others who never take the time to balance their checkbooks each month. Considering the high fees for overdrafts and late fees, it is much better economically to know exactly how much you have in the bank and when your bills are due.

If you already keep a complete record of all of your finances, you are ahead and can move on to the next section. For others, there are a number of software programs that will help with personal finances; Quicken and Microsoft's Money are two of the better-known ones. If you don't have the money to buy the software, look into shareware. This is software that can be downloaded from the Internet. Some is free and others cost very little. It may take time to learn, but it could be worthwhile in the long run.

Whatever you do, don't let the thought of learning a software program keep you from doing this exercise. You can keep your records on a yellow legal pad and still learn where you stand financially. What is important is that you take the time to keep the records.

Monthly Bills

Sit down and list all of your bills. Break them down into categories that make sense to you, based on their initial amounts and current balances—secured (by some form of collateral such as a car or house) and unsecured (most credit card accounts, student loans, personal loans from family/friends); or short-term (can be paid off in one year or less), low-balance and long-term, high-balance (home mortgages, most car loans, student loans).

However you organize them, include the following information: balance, monthly payment, interest rate, and, if a debt, when it should be paid off. If you have revolving credit cards where you make only the minimum monthly payment, the payoff could be years away since you are basically paying only the finance charges.

It's also a good idea to add up the monthly payments so you will have a clear picture of the total of those bills.

Credit Status

If you haven't seen a copy of your credit report recently, now may be a good time to get copies from the three major credit bureaus and check them over.

- How does your credit look?

- Have you made all of your payments on time?

- Do you have any delinquent accounts?

- Have you had to declare bankruptcy? If so, how long ago?

- Are there any mistakes on your reports? If so, contact the bureaus and file a letter of dispute.

Assets

List any assets you have: cash in the bank, savings accounts, certificates of deposit, or money markets, stocks, etc. What about equity in your home? Is it nearly paid for or have you purchased it within the last five years? Look into the current interest rates; you may be able to refinance your mortgage and save on your monthly payment and interest fees. Include other assets, such as vehicles that are paid for, boats, recreational vehicles, and real estate other than your home, such as rental property or a second home.

Net Worth

Determine a realistic value for each of your assets and total them up. Add up your liabilities or debts. Subtract your total liabilities from your total assets and you will find your net worth. Hopefully, it will be a positive number. This is a very simple way of determining your worth, and it can give you an idea of where you stand. If your finances are more complicated, you might approach someone you trust and respect who is knowledgeable enough in financial matters to help you.

Financial Alternatives

If you are currently employed, write down your take-home pay. If you are married or living with a significant other, include that person's income. If you are still employed, but having health problems, you may have already begun to wonder whether you can afford to change jobs, take some time off, or cut down on your working hours. If so, you are a step or two ahead.

If you have money left over after paying your bills and necessary living expenses, is there any possibility that you can pay off some of the bills early? It may be worth your while, if there are smaller bills that you can get out of the way without putting too much pressure on yourself. This kind of decision should be included when you set out goals.

If you are the sole support of your household, you may or may not be able to consider paying off some bills. For some of you, you may be facing some serious financial problems because of missed work or because you have had to quit working. However, you still need to have a clear picture of your finances. If you had to quit work, contact all of your creditors and let them know your situation. It's not a good idea to keep them in the dark. They're much more likely to work with you if you contact them first and maintain contact.

You may have to consider credit counseling. If you do, go to the library or online and research the different services. Not all credit-counseling organizations are nonprofit. You need to know exactly what they are going to charge you for helping you and exactly how they are going to work with your creditors. Check with your local Better Business Bureau to see whether any complaints have been made against the companies you are considering.

Once you have an idea of your financial status, you will have a better idea of whether you can afford to cut down on the number of hours you work, change jobs, change career fields, or go back to college/university or to a vocational training program. You may also be able to apply for government-sponsored disability and vocational rehabilitation, or look into vocational rehabilitation on your own.

Vocational rehabilitation and training are covered in Chapter 8. Are you on Social Security disability now and feel you need to earn an income? Are you aware of the Ticket to Work program recently introduced by the Social Security Administration? See Chapter 8 for details on that program.

Although health care could be included in other sections, I have deliberately chosen to include it under finances. If you have a chronic illness and you don't have health-care insurance through your own or a spouse's employer or under a disability plan, it is very difficult to obtain the medicines to keep that illness under control. Even with Social Security disability, there is a two-year waiting period before Medicare covers you and that plan doesn't include medications.

What kind of health-care insurance do you have? Do you currently have health-care insurance through your job or your spouse's job? What are your options if you leave your existing employer? Are you familiar with the COBRA law, which enables you to keep your insurance coverage at the same cost plus a minor administrative fee, for a period of time (usually eighteen months) after you leave a job?

Although there are a lot of times when I complain about the Veterans Administration medical care system, I am truly thankful for it. If I hadn't been affected by physical fitness tests in 1969 and received a medical discharge from the navy, I wouldn't have any medical care coverage today. My medicine alone would probably run between $250 and $300 a month and my doctors' visits and tests would add additional expense. An electric wheelchair costs $5,000 if purchased without any help, and the lift to fit it into my van was around $1,200.

On one of the disabilities forums on the Internet, someone made the comment that if an item, such as a battery for an electric wheelchair, is indicated for use for those with disabilities, it is bound to cost a lot more than a similar item that was for general public use. I can't prove his theory, but I do know that being disabled—with or without a chronic illness—is an expensive situation.

Physical World

Ask yourself the following questions:

- Where do you live—urban area, city, town, or rural area?

- Do you live in an apartment, single-family dwelling, duplex, or townhouse?

- Are you restricted to your current home, because of either a current mortgage or a spouse's job?

- Could you move to another place if you had to, for either training or new job opportunities?

- Is there something about your current home that would lend itself to some form of self-employment?

- If you live in a small town, does it provide you with a cheaper cost of living that might outweigh the advantages of moving to a larger town or city?

- Could you sell your home and move into something smaller that might cost less or be easier to maintain?

- Do you have access to adequate transportation, either a private vehicle or public transportation?

- If you have a problem with mobility and need assistance getting around physically, will you still be able to rely on transportation to a new job?

- How easy is it for you to get around your present home? Are there stairs to a second floor that you have difficulty using? If you use a wheelchair/scooter, do you have a ramp so you can get it into your home? Can you get around inside your home with your wheelchair if you use one?

Until I developed peripheral neuropathy in my feet, I could walk around my home except on my worst flare-up days. I couldn't stand very long or do much walking, but I could do most of my light housekeeping. When the neuropathy started, any weight on my feet caused severe pain, so I had to start using my Pride Sidekick electric scooter in the house. But it was too big to get through the doorways into my bedroom and my office without tearing up the doorframes. A friend and I removed the molding from the doorframes to my bedroom and my office. I still couldn't get into the third bedroom of the house on the scooter at all. I also had a lot of trouble getting into the refrigerator and freezer as well as trying to do the laundry.

The Veterans Administration provided me with one of the smallest Pride Jazzy model electric wheelchairs. I still have only an inch or two of clearance to get through the doorways into my bedroom and office, but I can get in and out without doing three-point turnarounds. The Jazzy will turn completely around on its axis with a fairly small turning radius. The majority of my furniture bears the marks where I have accidentally hit it with either the scooter or the chair. But I can do the laundry (except for hanging up the clothes) and I can get into the refrigerator. (You have to have some priorities, after all.) I still need to do something about widening the doorways, lowering the thermostat where I can reach it, and building small ramps for the doorsills for both the back door, which has the long ramp up to the door, and the front door, so I can go out on my front porch.

It is important to take into consideration your physical world in light of your limitations. If you are going to be making some changes, you need to look at every part of your life so that you can make your life as hassle-free as possible. Some features in a home that would only be minor inconveniences if you are healthy become major hassles when you must deal with health problems.

Social Life

I am using the term *social* here to apply to both family and friends. Are you married, engaged, separated? Are you the sole support of young children? Do you have adult children or dependent parents? Are they nearby? In the same community, town, city, or state?

We are social creatures, needing at least some contact with other people. Some personality tests you can take to help learn about yourself are suggested in Chapter 2. Most of us generally have a pretty good idea whether we are outgoing extroverts who must be around a lot of people frequently or we prefer to spend time with just a close friend or family member, or even if we like to spend time in solitary pursuits.

Often our social needs are met with our families and through those with whom we work or go to school. If you don't have family nearby, do you have a circle of friends? Everyone needs someone in their life. If you find it difficult to keep up with the pace of your "healthy" friends, make use of the telephone or the Internet to stay in touch. Try to get out of the house occasionally if you don't work. Contact with others adds to your mental good health. Try to meet someone for lunch or even a cup of coffee. It doesn't have to be an expensive outing.

Fatigue is a major problem with many CIs and individuals often find themselves cutting out activities until they are down to the bare

bones—usually going to their job, especially if they are the sole support of themselves and/or their family, and just the minimum they
must do to keep the household running. Hard as it is to do, it is still
important to keep some sort of social life.

I am divorced, with no children, and I live alone—with five cats.
With my low energy level and tight finances, I find it hard to justify
getting out. However, I do go to the mall right after the first of the
month to pay some of my bills in person and take the time to eat at
El Chico's Mexican restaurant, which is inside the mall. I've been
doing it so long now that the hostess, the restaurant manager, and
several of the longtime waiters know me and know that I always eat
the chicken enchiladas with sour cream sauce, rice, and beans—with
no jalapeno peppers. I enjoy the meal very much. Also, I have a
couple of friends whom I meet for lunch whenever their schedules
allow. One teaches high school French and the other is a college
adjunct instructor.

Several years ago, I went through both the Denton Citizens' Police and Fire Academies and I am an active member of the Citizens
Police Academy Alumni Association. When I became so depressed
after switching to the electric wheelchair in May 2001, I started
going down to the police department one day a week to enter information from pawn tickets into their computers. I could feel the difference in my mental attitude within a couple of weeks. This
particular job isn't very exciting, but it is one that needs to be done
and the officers appreciate the help.

If you don't have close friends or it's difficult to get together with
them, find a way to volunteer. Helping someone else helps you as
well.

Support System

Do you have a support system in place? In this case, I don't mean a
financial one, but an emotional one. Many people with CIs have
informal or formal support. The most obvious support should come
from a spouse and/or family, whether parents or children, brothers,
sisters, or other relatives. The operative word here is *should.*

Very often, when a spouse develops a CI, especially if it is severe,
a husband or wife is there for the spouse emotionally in the beginning. However, when it becomes clear that the condition is permanent, it is sometimes difficult for the healthy spouse to be able to
handle the changed conditions of the marriage. This is particularly

true if the couple has been very active physically, but now one partner can no longer participate in those strenuous activities.

I have heard this situation compared to an "implied contract." When the couple fell in love and began to consider marriage, there were certain unwritten, and often unspoken, expectations. There was an "implied contract" that this was how their married life would be lived. And now, with the advent of arthritis or a heart condition or multiple sclerosis, that contract has been broken. This isn't something that can be blamed upon the ill partner, but the healthy partner may still place blame, consciously or unconsciously.

A husband or wife who feels resentment at the limitations will have a hard time providing emotional support. In some cases, the marriage crumbles under the stress of coping with the illness. In others, the marriage is strengthened. It is very hard to know in advance how any marriage will react to the stress. So look at your support system along with the rest of your world, and see if there are ways to strengthen it, because it will be a big help for your efforts to work.

One of the hardest things I had to learn about living with a CI was to ask for help and to accept it when it was offered. I have always been extremely independent and self-sufficient. I didn't want to ask anyone for help, but I found that it is indeed a blessing to receive as well as to give. And I have seen the blessings that others have received when they have helped me. So often I have found strangers who have not only opened doors, but also taken items off top shelves or loaded items in my car for me.

There is nothing wrong with needing and receiving help. If you have the type of relationship with your family that allows you to ask and for them to give, whether it is taking you to a doctor's appointment, babysitting your child, or carrying in your groceries, accept it with a smile and pass it on to someone else down the line. There is always someone else who will need assistance, even if it is just a friendly smile to brighten his day.

It is important that your family and friends have an understanding of your CI, to give them a better grasp of what you are going through. This is true in cases of "invisible" disabilities, such as cardiovascular disease, diabetes, FM, lupus, and chronic fatigue, as well as the more obvious chronic illnesses like rheumatoid arthritis. Pass on the educational materials if others indicate their willingness to learn about your illness. Don't force it and don't harangue others; you will generally be able to tell who is interested. And remember, CIs do not impact just the individual with the illness; they impact the entire family, whatever the size of that family.

A more formal support group is usually found with others who have the same or a similar type of CI. These support groups can be tied to a number of different bases ranging from ones organized by other individuals in the same geographic region with the same illness to Internet forums or bulletin boards open to anyone interested in the illness. Sometimes the groups are sponsored by a national organization such as the Arthritis Foundation, or by a local hospital or health-care provider.

There are definite advantages to belonging to a support group. The individual finds out she is not alone. Information on the illness, treatment, and coping tips can be shared. The members also can find someone to talk to when they are feeling particularly down. In the majority of the cases, the information that is passed on is accurate and helps the individual take the first step in self-management of her illness.

Unfortunately, the opposite can also be true. Because chronic illnesses are not readily cured, individuals sometimes become desperate for a cure. This often leaves them susceptible to any salesperson with the "latest special treatment." Quackery has been around for a long time, probably as long as illness has. Up until the last few years, anything that was not recognized and approved by traditional Western medical practitioners was considered quackery. Now, alternative treatments are being actively considered, especially with such hard-to-treat illnesses as FM and CFS. The National Institutes of Health recently added a National Center for Complementary and Alternative Medicine to evaluate many of the treatments that are being offered. Acupuncture was one of the first treatments to be recognized as being helpful for certain conditions. Others are being studied to determine just how effective they are.

Another negative for support groups is that sometimes they turn into "pity parties" with nothing positive being shared among the members. The ideal would be for the members to provide helpful tips in coping and living with the illness, but sometimes that gets lost along the way. Instead, everyone seems intent on spending the time complaining, or one or two individuals will try to take control of the meeting for their own personal gripe sessions. It is up to the leaders of the group to prevent this from happening. It is also helpful to have a member of the health-care profession assist in evaluating any information that is passed on to the members. That could prevent personal beliefs from controlling any possible information on treatment and help prevent the inclusion of any highly questionable material.

The Internet has opened up a whole new world of possibilities for not only finding others to share experiences with, but also for disseminating information about specific illnesses, from diagnosis to treatment and prognosis. In fact, there is now so much information available that it is often hard to weed out the incorrect and that which could be downright harmful to those who are seeking help for their illness.

Go onto the Internet and search for any particular illness and there are likely to be thousands of hits (results from Web sites to references to the subject within Web sites). Quite often there will be numerous duplicates, including Web sites that are no longer active or that haven't been updated for several years. Search engines have become more selective, but the average Web surfer will simply use one of the standards, such as Yahoo!, Google, AltaVista, or Lycos. With the recent shakeout in the Internet sites, some of these may no longer be active when you read this book. So, how do you find the information, and how do you find a support group that you can trust?

A good idea is to try the federal government's basic beginning Web site, www.first.gov, and follow the links to health or disabilities. They will usually lead you to a list of organizations that may sponsor support groups, such as the Arthritis Foundation or the American Cancer Society.

Another option, as of this writing, is www.about.com, which has several hundred Web sites with human guides on subjects ranging from health matters and specific diseases such as arthritis to topics such as the U.S. government. Be sure to check for the latest information; many sites give a date when they were last updated, and remember that several months will have passed between the time I am writing this and the date when the book is printed.

At About.com each site also has forums where individuals can post messages for all to read and respond. Topics under a particular illness may include treatment, a particular medication, disability issues, frustrations of living with the illness, reactions to relevant news of the day, and even a simple "I need a hug today." The guides strive to keep blatant commercialism out of the forums as well as acting as monitors to forums. For many individuals who have had to quit work or restrict their activities, these forums or bulletin boards do work as a support system. There may come a time when you believe that you don't need to attend a support group on a regular basis, but it is good to know such a group is available if you need it.

Why should someone bother with a support system? Because, as I mentioned above, people need to know that they are not alone in their illness and that there are others out there who understand what they are going through. Support groups also generally provide good information on diagnosis, treatment, and coping skills.

Self-Management

Although this entire book could be considered self-management, I want to take the time to address the idea specifically. CIs often frustrate doctors and other health-care providers. With an acute illness or accident, there is a clear-cut diagnosis, treatment, and a fairly clear point of a return to good health or at least to the point of health that was present before the acute illness struck.

But CIs are often difficult to diagnose and treatment may or may not be clearly established by the medical profession. Many times, the only treatment available is an attempt to relieve the symptoms of the illness. Researchers are making great strides in finding the causes of many of today's chronic illnesses, but there is still a long way to go before a definite cure is found.

In the meantime, those of us with these frustrating, painful, often disabling illnesses must take charge of our lives. Prior to receiving a diagnosis, many people may go from one doctor to another in search of what is making them feel the way they do. If they are lucky, a diagnosis is made fairly quickly; if not, they are often left with the feeling that whatever the problem is, it is their fault.

Even with the first illness that I can really remember, rheumatic fever, I didn't get a diagnosis or treatment for nearly a year. It was only after my oldest sister had a heart attack caused by rheumatic fever at the age of 15 that I was taken back to the doctor for another look. I then missed nearly three months of school.

Most of the time in these last forty years, I haven't had a problem with routine health problems. However, it was seventeen years from the time the symptoms of my FM first appeared before I was correctly diagnosed. FM had not been an accepted illness until the late 1980s and it was 1990 when the American College of Rheumatology set forth the diagnostic criteria. Even today there are some doctors who do not believe that it exists, insisting instead that it is psychosomatic. None of the standard medical tests can confirm FM and some of the physiological changes that do occur with FM are found only by specialized tests, not normally conducted.

Treatment of FM, as well as of a number of other chronic illnesses, is for the symptoms. In the case of FM, the symptoms of chronic pain, fatigue, and disturbed sleep are treated. Often medicines must be adjusted or changed, added to other medicines in order to achieve some improvement. The frustration level for both patient and doctor can rise significantly before some improvement is seen.

Today patients insist on knowing more about their health and their illnesses and are taking a more active role in their management. I firmly believe that each person must take control of his health just as he does in other parts of his life. I'm not suggesting that you fire your doctor; instead join her as a partner. No one can live his life in a doctor's office or in a hospital. So you must become an active partner with your doctor and others in your health team and take responsibility for yourself.

Your doctor cannot be with you twenty-four hours a day, seven days a week. You are the one who must live in your body, the one who will be in pain, who will be exhausted, or who will have to strive to breathe through an asthma attack. So it is up to you to make sure that you take the medicine prescribed and then adjust your lifestyle to your illness.

Since the subject of this book is working, it is even more important to emphasize that if you are to be able to work, at whatever level possible, it is up to you to do whatever is necessary to control your CI. As an example, I have a nephew who has diabetes, which requires him to eat regularly; test his blood sugar on schedule; and, until recently, give himself injections of insulin. He now uses one of the implants that control the amount of insulin. He works as a corrections officer in a county jail facility in Florida. For many years, he ate what he wanted, forgot to check his blood sugar, and then would experience the problems that arise when diabetes is unchecked. He was literally taking his life in his own hands and when problems arose on jobs where he would nearly pass out, he was a danger to himself and to others around him if he were operating machinery.

Now, with his current job, he must always be alert and aware of what is going on around him and he is doing a much better job of managing his illness.

Whether your CI is one that may have a life-threatening element or not, I urge you to take control of and responsibility for your health. Learn as much as possible about it, ask your doctor questions, and if he brushes you off or suggests you leave everything to him, find another doctor. As I said earlier, you are the one who will be living—or dying—in your body, not the doctor. Managed health care has limited patients' choices in many ways and you will have to work within your health-care program.

Remember, if you do everything you can to keep your chronic illness under control, or at least as much under control as possible, then you can spend more energy on working.

Notes

1. Nathaniel Branden, *The Power of Self-Esteem: An Inspiring Look at Our Most Important Psychological Resource* (Deerfield Beach, Fla.: Health Communications, 1992), p. vii.

2. Nathaniel Branden, *How to Raise Your Self-Esteem* (New York: Bantam Books, 1988 reissue edition), p. 7.

CHAPTER Two

What Can I Do?
What Do I Know?

W hen you sit down to write a resume, you usually focus on two aspects of your background: your postsecondary education and your formal work experience. In this exercise, we are going to go beyond that. We are going to look at everything in your life that might be useful to you in finding a job or a self-employment/ small business opportunity.

Remember that not every skill or experience that we look at here will be right for this purpose. There may be some things that you really like to do, but they may not be feasible as a source of income. But this exercise may give you not just one possibility; it may offer you several options, and that's what makes it worthwhile to take the time to complete it. This exercise definitely takes some effort, but it also separates those who really, really want to find something to do from those who are just thinking about it.

I can say this because I first completed essentially the same exercise when I returned to college after a gap of several years. I applied to Governors State University, Chicago, and its Board of Governors Degree Program, which gave credit for life experience toward my bachelor's degree. Before I was accepted, I had to write down *every-thing* that I had done since I graduated from high school: work, school, training, volunteering, as well as leisure activities. I was in my midtwenties at the time and had served three years in the U.S. Navy as a journalist. After the service, I worked at several jobs before going back to college.

To complete this exercise today at age 54 would involve quite a bit more time and effort, but it would also show that I now have a great deal more to fall back on as possible sources of income. In the years when my health was getting progressively worse, I did much the same thing I am asking you to do, even though I didn't do it in a formal way.

My Work Background

Writing
- nonfiction book author
- newspaper editor
- newspaper reporter
- regional magazine writer
- local magazine publisher and editor
- newsletter editor and publisher
- creative writing instructor
- writing workshop coordinator
- copy editor

Photography
- newspaper photographer and editor
- portrait photographer
- school photographer
- industrial photographer

Teaching
- English tutor
- college adjunct instructor: English, American history, marketing, small business management, business communications, technical writing
- graduate teaching assistant
- high school librarian, journalism instructor, yearbook and school newspaper adviser
- GED tutor

Public Relations
- private businesses, nonprofit organizations, government agencies

Volunteer Coordinator
- nonprofit organization

Miscellaneous
- general office work
- temporary office work
- maid
- cashier
- waitress
- babysitter
- direct sales: cosmetics, jewelry
- nurse's aide

Crafts
- leather and wood maps and artwork
- greeting cards
- Western jewelry

The point is that everyone has a number of possibilities that can be pursued. In today's workforce, people change career fields on an average of three to four times during their working years and most of those changes have nothing to do with any disability. Many retired individuals often find they are bored with not working, and so they look around for an opportunity to work, often in a more flexible position or in a new field for them.

This chapter helps you determine what you know and, I hope, how much you know about a particular subject. Then, when you begin to look into the actual possibility of working, you will need to get a realistic picture of its money-making potential, either working for someone else in that field or being self-employed. You should also get a general idea of how much training you will need in order to get work. Training and education are discussed in detail in Chapter 8, but it is important to note that one of the biggest obstacles in hiring individuals with disabilities or limitations due to health is lack of skill in the field in which they are applying for work.

Formal Work Experience

The first step is to look at your formal work experience. If you are currently employed, write down the name of your employer, how long you have worked for the company or organization, and your job title. List all of the activities that you do in performing your job.

Job analysis is a process of breaking down a particular job into its essential functions or parts. This is a useful tool in interviewing, selecting, training, and promoting employees as well as in determining pay. Under the Americans with Disabilities Act, a person is considered to be qualified for a job if he or she can perform its essential functions, with or without accommodations. The Department of Labor has developed an excellent tool for job analysis. Although this job analysis is primarily for employers, it will help you look at all of the aspects of your job in the light of possible future employment.

The first step in a job analysis is to make a list of the tasks you perform at your current job (or your most recent job, if you are no longer employed). Ask yourself the following questions about each task:

Deciding What the Job Is[1]

1. How is the task performed? What methods, techniques, and tools are used?

2. How often is the task performed? Are the tasks performed less frequently as important to success as those done more frequently?

3. How much time is allotted to perform the task? Is the pace consistent?

4. Why is the task performed?

5. Where is the task performed?

6. How is success measured?

7. What happens if the task is done wrong?

8. What aptitudes are necessary? (Aptitude refers to the potential to learn and accomplish a skill.)

9. What knowledge is necessary? (Knowledge refers to the level of general or technical information.)

10. What skills are necessary? (Skills refer to the applied ability through training required.)

11. How much physical exertion is required? (Physical exertion refers to lifting, standing, bending, reaching, twisting, and crawling.)

12. What happens if the task is not completed on time?

13. What are the environmental conditions (i.e., hot, cold, dusty, wet, etc.)?

14. How much mental exertion is needed?

15. How much emotional exertion is needed?

By analyzing the job that you performed most recently, you should get a clear picture of the real physical and mental requirements of the job. How your chronic illness (CI) was affected by the physical activities of your job will help you determine the limitations you will face on a future job.

Now that you have seen what a formal job analysis looks like, use that as a model to describe all of your jobs and the activities that were included in each. If you had problems with the physical aspects of any part of your job(s), make a notation about that situation so that you will be able to compare it to the list you made of your physical limitations in Chapter 1.

When listing your formal work experience, be sure to include any special projects that went beyond your job description but that will add experience to your resume. For example, for several years I was the lifestyle editor for the Sun Journal newspapers in Lansing, Illinois. I was often called on to develop, write, edit, and lay out special sections for the papers, such as "Back to School," "Annual Progressive Business," and "Bridal," along with several others. Some of these went beyond my regular job requirements, while others were simply extensions of them. At night and on weekends, I also took family portraits, which were part of premium gifts given to new subscribers. Neither of these was in my formal job description, yet they each provided me with extra skills that I used several years later.

Education

Education is a standard listing on any job resume. Give your highest degree first, listing the name of the educational institution, the area of emphasis, and the date completed.

Formal

For example:

> MA, English, emphasis on creative writing, Governors State University, Park Forest South, IL, 1976

> BA, Board of Governors Degree, Communications, Governors State University, Park Forest, IL, 1974

You can also include education beyond the actual degrees you received, particularly if you have a significant number of hours toward a degree. So, I usually include this:

> MA, American History (except for thesis and foreign language), Midwestern State University, Wichita Falls, TX, 1983

Informal

Next comes the more informal part. Have you taken any specialty classes, through a local college or university, school district, or city parks and recreation department? Such classes could include things such as computer skills in word processing, database or Web publishing, photography, calligraphy, writing, foreign languages, or business management.

Your previous employer might have also provided training in certain areas to aid you in keeping up with your field or in learning new skills. If your company switched from one software program to another and your employer sent you to a seminar on the new software, that training would be something to include. Often employers also provide training in interpersonal relationships, teamwork, or even business communications for their employees that you could include. For example, the city of Denton, Texas, provides workshops for employees based on Stephen Covey's *The 7 Habits of Highly Effective People.*

Have you taken any other courses through home training or on-line classes? Although some of these might not be recognized officially, they may give you a step up in a job that requires skills related to that area. Have you attended any seminars or conferences that helped you learn a new skill or improve an old one? Many times such conferences will give continuing education credits. Such credits are not the same as a college course, but they do show employers that you are willing to take the time to learn.

Volunteer Work

It is not unusual for someone to move from a volunteer position to a paid position. Quite often the skills you have utilized as a volunteer can be transferred to a paid position. Does that mean that everything you have done as a volunteer will be suitable for you to use to obtain a job doing similar work? Not necessarily. It all depends upon how much experience you gained and whether there is a position that you can do within your physical limitations. And of course there must be a demand for that labor or service.

Let's look at some examples. Local United Way organizations work to raise money for the various groups that they help fund. They will quite often "borrow" employees from United Way member companies to help in their fund-raising campaigns. The companies will allow those employees to take time away from their jobs to speak to employees at other businesses about donating money. They may also take part in the actual planning of the fund-raising campaign. While these employees are volunteering as goodwill spokespersons, they are also developing public-speaking skills.

Many other nonprofit organizations also have to conduct fund-raising to support the organization's activity. This applies to almost any organization, from parent-teacher associations to such civic programs as Kiwanis, Lions, and Junior League. Although there is a big difference between raising funds for a parent-teacher association and a local United Way organization, or for a much larger regional or national organization, much of the process is the same; only the scale of needs and amount of money needed are different.

Another example of volunteer activity is working in a local library. While some volunteers may check out books or replace books on shelves, others may work with computers assisting patrons in researching material or in processing new books as they are received.

The list of possible volunteer jobs is almost as endless as the list of paid positions. For many nonprofit organizations, there are no funds for paid staff, because all money must go for the needs of the organization. Therefore, it is up to volunteers to perform these jobs. If you have ever volunteered in any way, you should include that in your list just as if it were a paid position.

Try to look at each volunteer position with an eye to how it could relate to future employment. The point is that you may utilize those skills for yourself in self-employment or small business, or in another position; you just have to find a proper place to put them to use. The skills are still the same. Were you a president, treasurer, newsletter editor, volunteer coordinator, or a disaster worker for an organization such as the American Red Cross or Salvation Army? Did you teach courses in safety, in computers or computer use, or hazardous materials cleanup?

Your chronic illness itself may even be a source of volunteer or paid work. There are many health conditions that have been recognized only in recent years and information on those conditions is hard to find. In the late 1980s and early 1990s, fibromyalgia (FM) and chronic fatigue syndrome (CFS) were still controversial diagnoses. Individuals with these conditions began to form local support groups and gradually several national groups arose. Several individuals with FM or CFS began to publish newsletters. One person in Arizona puts out a for-profit quarterly newsletter as well as several other publications and has been very active in raising awareness about the conditions.

I can again use myself as an example here. I received my diagnosis in late 1986 and began searching for answers to my questions on FM. My rheumatologist, Dr. Bernard Rubin of the Texas Osteopathic College in Fort Worth, Texas, finally told me, "You're a writer, write a book about it." I did, with Dr. Rubin as my coauthor. Although I have only used examples of FM and CFS, I have no doubt that other people are undergoing a similar experience with other diseases or health conditions.

Personal Interests, Knowledge, and Leisure Activities

This section can be as short or as long as your interests and activities. Some people have a number of areas of interest, while others have only a few, or none at all. For many with CIs, limited energy and the unpredictability of their symptoms may have restricted their involvement in activities outside of work. Sometimes, it becomes necessary to cut back on something you really care about, but you may not have to stop completely.

In 1991, I interviewed Jean Judy (at that time an occupational therapy instructor at Texas Woman's University) for the first edition of *When Muscle Pain Won't Go Away*. She suggested that if you can no longer do an activity that means a lot to you, find something that is related, but that is within your present limitations. For example, if your passion is horses, but you can no longer ride them, then photograph them, or publish a newsletter about them. Denton County, Texas, has a very large number of horse farms, and the highest population of horses in Texas. A local woman took advantage of that fact and developed a tour of the most prominent horse farms. Tourists as well as interested local residents make up her clientele. As far as I know she does not have a disability, but she has taken an interest in horses and turned it into a part-time business.

If you are interested in family histories, you may be able to do research within your county or region for those who can't travel to do it themselves. Even with all of the information on the Internet, someone still needs to do some local legwork. One of the good things about this type of work is that you can pace yourself.

So write down everything you are interested in; then narrow the list down to those things in which you would really like to be involved or about which you have the most knowledge. It is possible that you are very knowledgeable about a subject, but you really don't want to spend the amount of time on it that would be required to make money at it. Do you automatically scratch it off the list? That depends upon your goals, which we discuss in Chapter 3. It might be that you could work in an area part-time while you are preparing for a longer-term goal.

For example, you may do cross-stitch needlework and you are creative enough that you can design new patterns. There are computer software programs available to assist you both in designing the patterns and in creating a catalog to offer them for sale. Sales can be handled by mail order or orders can be taken from shop owners at a national or regional trade show. This could bring in money while you studied for some other business or job, or it could become your primary source of income. The same idea applies to many other forms of crafts or products.

Many serious craftspersons work throughout the year creating their products and then sell them the last three months of the year for the holidays. For example, one woman I interviewed paints and fires ceramic ornaments. She fills her own molds, paints them, and then fires them in her own kiln. It takes her about an hour to paint each one. She also creates other ornaments and then sells them at local craft shows and some home parties. She has a full-time job, so this is a way to earn Christmas money. For others, depending on their energy level, it could bring in more, based upon the amount of money and time they want to invest in it as well as the market for the product in a given area.

What if you have a subject in which you are interested but aren't knowledgeable enough about it that you feel you could make money at it? How do you learn more? That is something that is covered in Chapters 8 and 9.

Learning More About Yourself

When you are considering a career or a job that you can do with your limitations, how do you know whether you will be good at it? Do you have the type of personality traits that will help you succeed at your own business? By sitting down and thinking about what you did at your previous jobs or the activities involved in other areas of interest that you have looked at in this chapter, you can come up with a fair idea of what you have done and the possibilities you face. Now ask yourself the following questions:

1. What did you do well?

2. What did you enjoy the most?

3. What activity brought you compliments from your supervisors, coworkers, family, or friends?

4. Did you enjoy interacting with customers or clients?

5. Were you a self-starter? (Are you still?)

6. Did you work best alone, with few distractions?

7. Was it hard for you to concentrate and be productive in a noisy environment?

8. Did you prefer working inside or outdoors?

9. Do you think of yourself as outgoing or shy?

10. Did you like to use the telephone in your business?

11. Did you prefer to have a physical finished product as tangible evidence of your work or did you enjoy more intellectual activities?

Personality Type Tests

What happens if you cannot return to your previous employment and you don't have any definite interests that are realistic money-makers? What if you must completely change fields? There are dozens of books available as well as Web sites where you can take quizzes to help you if you are uncertain about what you want to do; see Appendix A for some suggestions.

One idea is to check out your personality type. Personality types or temperaments have been discussed since Hippocrates. Carl Jung developed a theory of psychological types based on our preferences for how we "function." In the 1950s, Isabel Myers and her mother, Katheryn Briggs, took Jung's theory and developed the Myers-Briggs Type Indicator. This divided everyone into sixteen personality types and has become a respected tool for psychologists and other professionals, as well as individuals.

The Myers-Briggs Type Indicator test can be taken under the guidance of a counselor or psychologist and is also available online for a fee. Although such a test is not necessary for you to understand what you would be good at, it is a good tool and may prove helpful. If you choose to take the Myers-Briggs or a similar personality quiz, contact the counseling office of your local college or university. You may also want to read some of the books listed in the resource section in Appendix A. Two examples are *Do What You Are: Discover the Perfect Career for You Through the Secrets of Personality Type*, by Paul

D. Tieger and Barbara Barron-Tieger, and *Please Understand Me II, Temperament, Character, and Intelligence*, by David Keirsey. They are both very good resources if you cannot afford to take the Briggs-Myers test.

There are a number of other personality tests that you can look into. Many are available online with interpretations to help you understand the results. Some are free and others have a fee.

Career Guidance Tests

What about a career guidance test? How is it different from a personality test? Again, this is a personal choice for you. You don't have to take any of the tests or quizzes if you feel that you have a good idea of what you want to do and what you are comfortable doing. There are two types of career guidance tests: those that identify your interests and those that identify your aptitude or abilities in various subjects.

Most of us are familiar with the career interest tests that ask us whether we would prefer to work outdoors or indoors. This is similar to the questions with which I started this section. The aptitude test will let you know whether you are weak in, say, math. You definitely would not want to go into bookkeeping or accounting if that were the case. What if your highest scores were in communication skills and written comprehension? This could lead you to such fields as teaching or writing.

You may already be comfortable enough in knowing what you are good at. If that is the case, you do not have to take the time to follow up on this idea. If you choose to pursue the tests or quizzes, see Appendix A for more suggestions.

Next Steps

Perhaps you are in the process of finding work that you can perform within the limits of your chronic illness. Whatever you choose to do, whatever career, job change, or part-time work you select, you want it to be something that you enjoy, something that will bring you a sense of satisfaction, not drag you down physically, mentally, or emotionally. I urge you to take the time to do all that you can to provide yourself with sufficient information so you can make the best decision.

If you are facing financial problems and the need to bring in money as soon as possible, do what is necessary to find the funds. However, don't stop at that. Keep in mind the exercises in this book and the goals we discuss in Chapter 3. There are short-, medium-, and long-term goals. Your short-term goal will be to make some money now; your long-term goal will be to find the work you love that will also bring you the satisfaction and the financial rewards you deserve.

All too often, we feel that we must settle for whatever we can get, whatever job we can find or be hired for. I know the reality of the world and the economic hardships that we face all too often. But in the long run, you don't have to settle for anything less than what you really want to do. Do your homework, find the work you want to do and can do, then reap the satisfaction of once more being a productive individual.

Note

1. U.S. Department of Labor, Office of Disability Employment Policy Fact Sheet, "Ready, Willing, and Able." www.dol.gov/dol/odep/public/media/reports/rwa00/toc.htm.

Three

Goal Setting: Where Do I Want to Go, What Do I Want to Do?

In the introduction and the first two chapters, we looked at chronic illnesses (CIs) in general, as well as at your CI and its impact on you. Then we looked at your overall situation, from your finances to your work experience and your interests. If you chose, you took some personality quizzes and/or career guidance tests. The next step is to set up some goals. You need to know what you want to do, what you want to accomplish, and where you want to be in the immediate future, within five years, and in the long term.

Being Realistic and Flexible in the Face of Uncertainty

Goal setting for those with the limitations of CI is a bit different from goal setting for everyone else. You must always take into account those limitations. Although I advocate reality for everyone when I teach goal setting, it is even more important to those with a CI.

Because the symptoms of many CIs vary from one day to the next, the amount of energy you'll have available to meet your goals is also uncertain. One of the most frustrating parts of living with a chronic illness is the uncertainty—making plans can become a source of stress in itself. Far too often, we make plans to go somewhere, to take part in some activity either as an individual or as a family, only to find out on the day of the event that we have no energy or that the symptoms of our CI have flared up and it is impossible to do what we planned.

I have heard so many men and women talk about the disappointment, not only theirs but also their family's, when they just couldn't carry out their plans. If you can't know from a few days to a week or more in advance whether you will be able to do something, how can you set any goals? How can you hope to accomplish them? This is probably the hardest part of the process that I am offering you in this book. Because none of us can tell the future, none of us can really tell what will happen or how we will feel, physically or mentally, in either the near or far future.

Do I have a magic pill or spell or formula to ensure that you will be able to meet your goals? No, but I wish I did, because I'd be the first to take it or use it. I often feel that if I had my health back, I would set the world on fire, writing book after book. But I am a realist (my personality quizzes agree), and I know that I must live with the cards I've been dealt. There may be a cure for fibromyalgia (FM) someday, but I don't expect it to happen soon enough to do me any good, and so I plan my life accordingly.

Whatever your CI, you should educate yourself about it, its symptoms, treatment, and prognosis. I don't want you to focus on the downside or the negative aspects; you just need to know what the possibilities are, then do everything within your power to manage your health and your life to live as fully as you can. If we take care of ourselves, then will we be able to count on meeting our goals? Yes, if we are flexible. If there is one word that we need to remember with regard to CI, it is *flexible*. Whenever possible, we must be flexible in our scheduling and in what we are doing.

Will an employer be flexible? There are many who are. One of the women who responded to my request for input reported that her boss allowed her to take work home or to change her working hours based on how she was feeling. Even at a time when the economy is uncertain and many companies are tightening their belts, they seem to be keeping flexible working schedules. A recent article in the *Denton Record-Chronicle* covered many of the perks that companies are now cutting. But it also discussed the flexible scheduling options available at Texas Instruments, Inc., such as that used by employee Marla Finco. She starts work at 5 A.M. so she can leave in the early afternoon to look after her young child.[1] Flexible work scheduling is one of the accommodations suggested by the Job Accommodation Network (JAN) for many of those with chronic illnesses and disabilities. Many of the accommodations that JAN suggests do not involve expensive changes; some examples of these accommodations are discussed in Chapter 6.

Sometimes a flexible work schedule or telecommuting is not always possible because of the particular demands of a specific job. There are some tasks that must be done on a tight schedule, or jobs that must be done in a particular location, something you must keep in mind when you are looking for work. However, many employers are allowing employees to telecommute, and it's not only because they have an illness or disability. In fact, legislation has been reintroduced in the House of Representatives, as of this writing, that would offer a $500 tax credit for either companies or individuals "for expenses paid or incurred under a teleworking arrangement for furnishings and electronic information equipment which are used to enable an individual to telework." The idea is to increase the number of Americans who telework and decrease the number of vehicles on the roads, thus reducing traffic congestion and air pollution.

A 1999 Telework America National Telework Survey, conducted by Joan H. Pratt Associates, found that the 19.6 million telecommuters often work up to nine days a month from home. According to experts, 40 percent of the nation's jobs are compatible with telework. The Telework Tax Incentive Act cosponsored by Senator Rick Santorum (R, Pa.) and Congressman Frank Wolf (R, Va./10th) will encourage telecommuting. Senator Santorum made the following statement in a press release dated March 13, 2001, and released by his press office: "Telecommuting improves the quality of life for everyone by reducing traffic congestion, air pollution, gas consumption and our dependence on foreign oil. In addition, telecommuting gives working parents more choices and increased flexibility to meet the everyday demands of their family, and provides *greater job opportunities for disabled members of the work force*." [Emphasis added]

It is important to note the difference between "telework" and "telecommuting." Telecommuting generally refers to the practice of allowing current employees of a company to work in a location other than their primary workplace for a portion of their work schedule. This work may be done at home or at a remote telework center or satellite office. You are more likely to be able to persuade your current employer to arrange a telecommuting setup than to find a job that allows you to stay at home. One aftermath of the September 11 terrorist attacks is that there seems to be an increase in the number of companies that are either adopting telecommuting or allowing more employees to telecommute.

Because the term *telework* is sometimes applied to both telework centers and satellite offices, it can create confusion. A telework center is generally an office set up as an independent business, and it provides a facility where individuals can come together to work, either using the facility's computers or bringing their own laptops. These facilities are usually located in suburban areas and serve those who live nearby.

A satellite office is one that a particular company has leased or built in an area where a number of their employees are located. The employees who live in that area can then report to work at the satellite office rather than commuting to the primary facility.

An individual can be a teleworker in a number of ways, but the primary distinction between teleworkers and telecommuters is that the teleworker is self-employed and works freelance for various clients, rather than for one employer. The individual is responsible for purchasing and maintaining her home office, including obtaining and maintaining whatever telecommunication or other equipment might be necessary to perform work for her clients.

The Four P's

Jean Judy, the occupational therapist I interviewed for my book on FM, emphasized what she calls the four P's: planning, pacing, playing, and priorities.

Planning

Planning is an absolute necessity when living with CI. Planning allows you to conserve energy as well as time. I am a great list maker and I love yellow legal pads. I have legal pads on clipboards for my "to do" lists. I make a list of housework, of errands to run (so I won't forget to go somewhere), even major projects that I want to take on. When my energy is at its lowest, planning out what just has to be done and how it can be done with the least amount of energy expended is vital. Even though I'm now in a wheelchair, I still try to make sure that I carry whatever I may need when I go from one end of my home to the other. Seventy-six feet doesn't sound like a long way until you've had to make the trip three times because you forgot to take something that you needed when you got to either end of the house. Needless to say, I make lots of lists and do a great deal of planning when I am writing.

Pacing

When I discussed the uncertainty of a chronic illness, I urged you to be flexible. Pacing means listening to your body and stopping for a rest when you need it. Of the many problems that people talk about in coping with their CI, pacing is the one that gives them the most trouble. I have to confess that I am probably the world's worst about pacing myself. When I become engrossed in a writing project, I can lose all track of time. I hate to stop, either for a brief rest or for the day. But I always pay the price because I pushed myself too hard.

With many chronic illnesses, the symptoms may come and go. Some days you feel great and others you feel lousy. Unfortunately, because we have so many days when we feel lousy and don't accomplish anything, we have a tendency to overdo when we feel good, so pacing is important.

Playing

When you set your goals, make sure that you set aside some time for play. It is very hard to do when you have so little energy and so much that needs to be done. However, you will find that taking the time to play, at whatever activities you find relaxing or enjoyable, will give you more energy in the long run. Everyone needs to "recharge their batteries," and play allows you to do that.

Priorities

When looking at your life with CI, you may feel that all you can manage is trying to support yourself, if you are single, or you and your dependents, if you are the head of a household. In a July 24, 2001, press release, the National Organization on Disability presented a look at those individuals with disabilities who took part in its survey. The survey found that there are more individuals with disabilities who live alone or are single parents than who live with spouses. The large number of aging baby boomers may be responsible not only for dependent children, but also dependent parents. And the numbers of individuals with chronic illnesses and disabilities is expected to increase as those baby boomers age. How can a person find time for his dependents, go to work, maintain a household, and manage his own personal care within the limits of his energy and abilities? He must learn how to prioritize.

When I learned how to clean house, I was taught to move the stove and refrigerator out and clean under them on a regular basis. Also, in order to get kitchen and bathroom floors really clean, I would often be on my hands and knees scrubbing at stubborn stains. Every time I did this, I had a flare-up, and several times it cost me my jobs because it would take two or three months before I could work again. I finally decided that my floors didn't need to be that clean and I would only clean under the stove and refrigerator when I was getting a new appliance or moving. I established some priorities; working at a job was more important than having a sparkling clean kitchen floor. Most of us do this sort of thing automatically. I want you to do it deliberately and in all of the areas of your life that we have been looking at.

Ask yourself these questions:

- What is your number one priority?

- What has to take front and center of your attention and your energy?

- Are you bringing in enough money to support yourself or yourself and your dependents?

- Do you have enough income so that you can provide some extras for your children?

- Does your family need your income to make ends meet or to save for your children's college expenses?

- Do you want to find work that will bring you a sense of fulfillment as well as an income?

- Have you reached a point in controlling the symptoms of your CI where you now feel the need to reach out to others?

- Are you feeling left behind with the world moving past you outside your door?

It is important that you know what you *must* do as well as what you *want* to do. Sometimes we are lucky and they are the same thing; other times, we do what we must and what we want has to wait.

Take the time now to decide what you want or need in each area of your life and set up some goals.

What Are Goals and Why Should I Bother with Them?

Goal setting is important because it gives you something specific to work toward and to give structure to your plans. Goals fall into three general categories: short range or immediate (can be completed within the next year), intermediate (may take up to five years to achieve), and long range (will probably take ten years or longer to accomplish). Once you set your goals, you should create a list of objectives that will help you achieve your goals. Think of them as steps toward the goals. As you write your lists, keep the following factors in mind.

Realistic

Goals must be *realistic* if they are going to work. You might aspire to be an astronaut, but if you are now fifty years old and have a severe health condition, it's not a realistic goal. And, yes, I know about a certain very, very rich, older gentleman who bought his way into space. Most of us are not going to be able to do what he did.

Achievable

Your goals should also be *achievable*. Does that mean you can't dream big? No. Just make sure that your dreams are within reach. Don't set them too low, either, for then there is no challenge. You might think that just finding a job should be a goal in itself, that it doesn't matter what you are doing as long as you are earning some money, and that finding an employer who will work with you is all you can expect. Don't settle for less than you are worth. You have something to offer prospective employers. Don't take a job just because it is the first one offered to you. Make sure it is something you will enjoy doing.

Acknowledge the limitations that you have, but don't let them set the value on your worth as a contributing employee. You have your own knowledge and skills to offer.

Measurable

Goals must be *measurable*. To say that you want to be rich doesn't have any meaning. What is rich? How much money does it take to be rich? Do you need $20,000, $100,000, or a million dollars?

The Texas State Lottery Commission found that sales of lottery tickets dropped significantly when the prize was $4 million, the lowest amount in the biweekly lottery drawings. So it produced some television commercials showing individuals receiving $4 million. The actors would just throw the check in a drawer as if it was "no big deal." The fact is that for most of us $4 million would mean we were rich. For someone among the group of the top richest people in the United States, it wouldn't have the same meaning.

When you set a goal for yourself, make it measurable, and make it countable. If you don't, you may not know when you have reached that goal. How do *you* measure financial security, career success, and family or personal happiness? Only you know the answer to that, but you need to establish a goal that you will know when you have achieved it.

Specific

Goals must also be *specific* to you. They must be *your* goals. Don't let someone else dictate your goals. They must be something that you want for yourself or you won't work as hard to achieve them. How does that apply when you are considering family goals? Family life involves the fine art of balancing everyone's personalities, wants, and desires. It generally involves compromise. Hopefully you and your spouse can sit down together and develop goals for you as a couple and for the entire family.

It is also important that you set a specific time frame for achieving your goal; otherwise, you may keep putting it off and leave it for "some other day."

Whole-Life Goal Setting

Remember, it's important to keep in mind that we are looking at your whole life here, not just a job. You need to have a life that is as well rounded as possible because it contributes to your overall feeling of well-being. You also need to keep your stress levels—both good and bad—as low as possible. Some people don't realize that even when good things happen, they are under stress. Almost everyone with a CI is affected by stress, which tends to make the symptoms worse.

I believe in going further than what most people think about when setting goals. In looking at the whole person, not just a career, we will focus on setting goals in your personal, family, and financial areas as well as your career. Some may choose to add spiritual goals as well. Think of goal setting as building the life that you want to live, doing the things you want to do. Goals must be realistic, achievable, measurable, and specific. They must motivate you, and you must bear the responsibility of seeing them through. List objectives that will help you achieve your goals. Objectives are the steps that you need to take in order to achieve your goal. Each goal should include a time frame and a clear statement of the goal. Write down your goals and objectives to make them more real. In the pages that follow are some examples of goals in each of the areas discussed.

Personal

Set some personal goals for yourself. Is there something you would like to do "just for fun"? Perhaps you want to learn how to paint or to speak another language, or you'd like to go out and take photographs, not necessarily for money but for your own pleasure. It doesn't even have to cost money; it may just mean taking the time to go to the library by yourself one afternoon or one evening a week, or go to a city park. More and more parks and recreation areas are being made accessible even if you use a wheelchair or scooter. The following is an example of some personal goals:

Personal Goals

Goal One: Personal—Immediate
Find one hour a week for just you, to do with as you please, to relax or to energize yourself. Time frame: within the next two weeks.

> **Objective 1.** Look over all of the other demands on your time.

> **Objective 2.** Determine exactly what you want to do—or not do—for that hour.

> **Objective 3.** Set a specific time and place for that hour.

> **Objective 4.** Keep that appointment with yourself.

Goal Two: Personal—Short Range
"I want to volunteer with a group or organization where I will be productive and also feel that I am contributing something to my community at large." Time frame: one month.

(continued on page 54)

Objective 1. Look over your lists of interests and activities. Narrow that list down to ten possibilities, then down to five within one week.

Objective 2. Contact organizations that involve volunteers and that fit with your interests. Find out their needs and their requirements for volunteers. Are they flexible enough to take your limitations into account? Complete by the end of week two.

Objective 3. Narrow your choices down to three and attend a meeting, visit their building/office/location, by the end of week three.

Objective 4. Based upon the knowledge of their needs and yours, and your response to your visit with them, choose one and set a definite start date or sign up for training.

Example 1. You can volunteer with the library and read during the weekly children's story hour. You will need to commit for at least two months and can miss only twice during that time if you want to stay with the program.

Question: Do you really want to spend that time with children? Will you be able to keep your commitment each week for the two months?

Example 2. You can attend an upcoming Citizens Police Academy, which requires you to attend three-hour classes for a twelve-week period. You must attend at least ten classes in order to graduate. Afterward, you can join the CPA Alumni Association that meets monthly plus has volunteer opportunities such as Child ID registration at community events and special occasions. You can also assist in raising funds that will help buy needed items for some of the Police Department sections that are not in the city's budget.

Question: Is twelve weeks too long for a commitment right now? Can you handle a three-hour class after your daily activities? Will there be another class in the future when you might be in better shape to attend?

Family

Do you have goals for your family? Do you want a family? For someone with a CI, family goal planning is very important. It is also something that should be discussed with your doctor. Do you want to take a special vacation with your family that you will need to set aside more money for? Are there activities that you want your children to be able to participate in? Are there activities that you want to attend that are difficult right now because of accessibility? Here is an example of the steps you could take in setting a family goal:

Family Goals

Goal One: Family—Immediate
Plan for a family night out at a restaurant/fast food and activity. Time frame: one month.

Objective 1. Determine what your budget can handle in the way of a night out, and what you can handle with your CI limitations. Time frame: one week.

Objective 2. Check with other family members on what they would like to do, explaining the budget limitations. Time frame: second week.

Objective 3. Check out the choices family members have suggested and if necessary, check for accessibility. Then set a date with a "rain date" in case your CI acts up.

Objective 4. Go out and have fun.

Questions. Do we need this time together? Can we afford such a night/afternoon? Can everyone find one night when we can all be together? Who bears the responsibility of making sure this happens? Remember, this is supposed to be an enjoyable occasion, not a guilt trip or stressed-out time.

Financial

Since you are reading this book, I'm assuming that one of your goals is to find work that is compatible with your CI. So you can set that down as goal number one. Just what type of work, where, and when will be determined by some of the following goals. These goals will reflect your financial status, which you wrote down earlier.

- What is your immediate goal for your finances?

- Do you have to find work as soon as possible?

- Do you have time to search for a job?

- Do you need help finding a job?

- What do you need in terms of money in take-home pay? What are the possibilities for pay raises?

- What kind of benefits do you need to go with the money? Do you need health care, vacation time, and sick leave?

- Do you need to work for a company that provides on-site day care?

- Is it important that the business or organization pay completely or partially for college courses and additional training?

- Are you working now but need some sort of accommodations to help with the symptoms of your CI? Is your current employer open to working with you on those accommodations? (Remember that the law says an employer *must make* "reasonable accommodations" *if* you have a disability as defined by the Americans with Disabilities Act; see the overview of the American with Disabilities Act in Chapter 4.) Many employers will work to keep a good employee by making some accommodations.

- Are you now working but need to find a position that will accommodate your limitations better? Or is your employer not open to making accommodations, which forces you to find a company that will?

- Can you afford to work part-time or do you need to work full-time to bring in enough money to live on?

Financial Goals

Goal One: Financial—Immediate
Determine exactly where you stand with your finances using the steps described in Chapter 1.

Objective 1. Gather all bank statements, bills, and paycheck records. Time frame: one week.

Objective 2. Make sure checkbooks are balanced, and if you use a software program for your finances, make sure everything has been entered. If not, based upon the number of bills, checking and savings accounts, etc., set up a realistic time frame for entering the information.

Objective 3. If you don't use a computer for your financial record keeping, set up a simple system, such as the one described in Chapter 1, and write down everything, so that you know exactly where you stand financially. Set a realistic time frame for this.

Career

Financial and career goals are very closely linked, especially when you must deal with limitations caused by a CI. Many individuals who are dealing with their health problems often feel as if they have no choice about their career. However, as I've mentioned before, remember that you need to be working at something that you enjoy, that will bring in the money that you need, and that will present the least amount of stress possible.

So, what is your situation? Look at the following examples of situations to get an idea about where you are:

1. Your employer is open to options and wishes to keep you.

2. You are unemployed at present but would like to work.

3. You are employed, but your position needs more than minor changes to enable you to keep working.

4. You have been unemployed for several months and need a job in a new field, so additional training or education is necessary.

5. You are unemployed, and you must work because of finances, but your cognitive and physical limitations make this difficult.

6. You are currently employed, but you must come home and go to bed immediately, every night. If changing jobs, you can't afford any loss of income or loss of insurance benefits.

7. You are unemployed, and you have been turned down for Social Security disability benefits. You need work *now*, but pain and cognitive problems from both your condition and your medications make concentrating difficult.

When you have determined where you are in relation to any of the above situations, then decide where you want to go. Write down what you need right now, both in terms of money and in your career. If you have to do something immediately, that is your first goal. Here are two examples of career goals and the steps that can be taken to accomplish them:

Career Goals

Goal One: Career—Immediate
Find work that you can do within your limitations. Time frame: one month.

(continued on page 58)

Objective 1. Refer to the self-evaluation that you made in Chapter 1. In light of your limitations, your physical situation—which includes where you live, your access to transportation (whether private vehicle or public transportation), and your financial resources—think of what you can do.

Objective 2. Follow the job-hunting steps covered in Chapter 9.

Goal Two: Career—Short Range

Within six months you want to find a job that will meet the majority of the following criteria:

- You will earn $X take-home pay, with health insurance as one of the benefits.

- You will have a flexible schedule, which includes telecommuting two to three days a week.

- You will spend the majority of your time writing, but you will be able to utilize voice recognition software, a compatible digital recorder, and a lightweight keyboard for text writing.

- You will have a lot of freedom in scheduling your tasks, but with a recognized deadline for projects.

- The job will bring you a sense of accomplishment and pride in being productive.

Objective 1. Review your evaluation of work experience, education, and interests. Time frame: one week

Objective 2. Go to the library or online and review *Occupational Outlook*, published by the Department of Labor, specifically looking for the projections for jobs that involve writing and service. Determine the requirements in terms of education and experience for those jobs. Time frame: two weeks

Objective 3. Go online or contact the counseling office of the nearest college or university to see about taking personality type quizzes or career aptitude tests (find out costs, times, etc.). If available at convenient times/places and at a cost you can afford, schedule the one you feel you need most, based on your own experience and education. Time frame: one month (you may have to wait for a regular scheduled time for testing.)

Objective 4. Follow the tips offered in Chapter 9 on job hunting. Time frame: two to four months.

Objective 5. Find your ideal job, with appropriate accommodations, and enjoy it.

Training and/or Retraining

Consider the following questions:

- Do you need vocational training or other education before you can go back to work?

- Based on your education, can you find other work in a field that is close to the one you are working on now?

- Taking into consideration your evaluation of your world, your limitations, and your needs, do you want to find another job in a brand new field? Will you need to go back to college for such a job?

- Will you need financial aid for any new education, whether it is at the college level, vocational in nature, or highly specialized?

Now that you have an idea of where you want to go, it's time to find out what resources are available to you. The federal government has an enormous amount of information, assistance, and tips on resources beyond what it offers. One of the primary reasons for starting your research with the government is that almost everything is free. Your tax dollars have paid for this assistance, so take advantage of it. Part II gives you an overview of the government resources available to help you.

Note

1. Crayton Harrison, "Companies Cut Perks and Save," *Denton Record-Chronicle,* August 12, 2001, p. C16.

Government Employment Resources

CHAPTER Four

When Your Health Deserts You: Chronic Illness and the Law

It has never been easier to find information on programs and services available from the federal government. The government recently set up a Web site, http://www.first.gov, as the first stop on the Internet for the public. You can start there and click on the citizens link and then on disabilities, or you can go directly to http://www.disabilitydirect.gov for specific information on programs and laws for those with disabilities.

This is the open doorway to the many programs and services that can help you learn about your employment rights, including the rights protected under the Americans with Disabilities Act (ADA). The government also provides information that will help you make career decisions, and find out where you can get vocational rehabilitation and even financial assistance for further training.

How Far Have We Come?

In the introduction to this book, I discussed the idea of disability. The fact is that even our government does not have one definition for disability. If we look back at history, we find that society as a whole generally believed that disabilities were caused by sin. It was either the fault of the parents (the "sins of the fathers" visited against the children) or the sins of the individuals themselves.

Progress on how others see those with disabilities has been made, though some people might question that statement. Even today many individuals with chronic illnesses (CIs) are often told that they haven't "prayed hard enough" to be healed or that God is "testing their faith" by giving them a "burden to bear."

How far have we come from the days when imperfect babies were killed at birth or hidden away? How far have we come from the days when someone with a mental illness was accused of being possessed by a demon? Do we still ignore someone who has severe depression or, worse yet, tell him to "pull yourself out of it"?

When we look at it from this angle, we have come a long way, but despite the Americans with Disabilities Act and other equal opportunity laws, discrimination still occurs. I have experienced it because I use a wheelchair. A number of years ago, I was hired as an adjunct English instructor at Texas Woman's University. I had sent in my resume, which gave my education and the other colleges where I had taught English as well as other courses. I was hired over the telephone just before the semester started. This scenario is not uncommon, because universities and colleges don't always know whether they will have to add classes or pick up another adjunct instructor until the last minute.

When I spoke to the head of the department, we discussed my experience, and when he asked me to teach a class, I didn't even think about saying anything about the wheelchair. The man gave me the class information, where the room was located on campus, and an approximate number of my students. I immediately went to the campus to find the classroom. I didn't want to wait until the classes started the next week to try to find my way around. As it turned out, the handicapped parking spaces were just across the street from the building where the classroom was located, but I had to go down the block and through a convoluted route to get to the classroom itself because the main entrance was on an incline and had about ten steps up to the door.

After tracking the path I would have to take to get to the classroom, I went around to the English department to pick up my materials for the class, fill out the usual forms, and meet the head of the department. To this day, I can't remember whether he said anything about my chair or not; back then I didn't think about being discriminated against. If he was surprised to learn that I was disabled, he didn't say anything. However, after the semester was over, he refused to even take my phone calls, although he had originally talked about having me continue to teach classes when he hired me. My class evaluations, which are filled out by the students at the end of the semester, have always been very good and were for that class as well. I have often wondered why he would not even talk to me, and the occupational therapy instructor I had interviewed for my book on fibromyalgia made the comment that she felt it was because of the wheelchair. During the semester I taught there, I found out that I was the only instructor, full- or part-time, who used an aid for mobility, except for one instructor who had broken her leg. I have not been on campus since, except to use the library, nor have I talked to anyone about the experience and whether the situation has changed. I hope so. One interesting point about the experience is that the university has a very strong health-care department offering degrees in nursing and physical and occupational therapy.

Research by the National Rehabilitation Information Center showed that the use of mobility devices doubled from 1980 to 1990. The National Health Interview Survey found just over 6.8 million community-resident Americans use assistive devices. One fact that struck me personally was that "less than 20 percent of working-age wheelchair and walker users are employed while the employment rate for crutch users is more than twice as high."[1] Thankfully, North Central Texas College, formerly Cooke County Community College, had no reservations about me or about the wheelchair, and I was able to teach classes there before my fibromyalgia became worse and I had to stop any outside work.

The New Freedom Initiative

The New Freedom Initiative,[2] announced by President Bush on February 1, 2001, is part of a long-term, nationwide effort to remove barriers to community living for people with disabilities. It represents an important step in ensuring that all Americans have the opportunity to learn and develop skills, engage in productive work, make choices about their daily lives, and participate fully in community life. The New Freedom Initiative's goals are to:

- Increase access to assistive and universally designed technologies
- Expand educational opportunities
- Promote home ownership
- Integrate Americans with disabilities into the workforce

- Expand transportation options
- Promote full access to community life

In support of the New Freedom Initiative, the president issued Executive Order 13217 on June 18, 2001, which directs the Department of Health and Human Services (HHS), the Department of Housing and Urban Development (HUD), the Department of Education (DOE), the Department of Justice (DOJ), the Department of Labor (DOL), and the Social Security Administration (SSA) to:

- Work collaboratively with each other to help states achieve the goals of Title II of the Americans with Disabilities Act (ADA).
- Ensure that existing federal resources are used in the most effective manner to swiftly implement the Olmstead decision and support the goals of the ADA.
- Evaluate the policies, programs, statutes, and regulations of their respective agencies to determine whether any should be revised or modified to improve the availability of community-based services for qualified individuals with disabilities.
- Ensure that each agency's self evaluation includes input from consumers, advocacy organizations, providers, and other relevant agencies.[3]

The New Freedom Initiative encompasses many areas of the ADA that will have an impact on those whose primary concern is employment. It is supposed to increase funding and assistance in the areas of education and transportation as well as assistive technologies.

Americans with Disabilities Act

The ADA prohibits discrimination against people with disabilities in employment, transportation, public accommodation, communications, and activities of state and local government. The law was passed in 1990 and became effective in stages:

- Businesses with twenty-five or more workers, as of July 26, 1992
- Employers with fifteen or more workers, as of July 26, 1994
- State and local government activities, as of January 26, 1992
- Public accommodations in compliance as of January 26, 1992
- Transportation phase-ins for accessibility from thirty days to thirty years

Although more people are now aware of the ADA than they had been over the last decade, many employers and even individuals with disabilities do not really know much about it or its purpose. Some important portions of the law are excerpted and discussed in this chapter.[4] Let's start with the findings of Congress that led to the establishment of the law in the first place. Remember that the figures used were pre-1990.

a) Findings.—The Congress finds that—

(1) some 43,000,000 Americans have one or more physical or mental disabilities, and this number is increasing as the population as a whole is growing older;

(2) historically, society has tended to isolate and segregate individuals with disabilities, and, despite some improvements, such forms of discrimination against individuals with disabilities continue to be a serious and pervasive social problem;

(3) discrimination against individuals with disabilities persists in such critical areas as employment, housing, public accommodations, education, transportation, communication, recreation, institutionalization, health services, voting, and access to public services;

(4) unlike individuals who have experienced discrimination on the basis of race, color, sex, national origin, religion, or age, individuals who have experienced discrimination on the basis of disability have often had no legal recourse to redress such discrimination;

(5) individuals with disabilities continually encounter various forms of discrimination, including outright intentional exclusion, the discriminatory effects of architectural, transportation, and communication barriers, overprotective rules and policies, failure to make modifications to existing facilities and practices, exclusionary qualification standards and criteria, segregation, and relegation to lesser services, programs, activities, benefits, jobs, or other opportunities;

(6) census data, national polls, and other studies have documented that people with disabilities, as a group, occupy an inferior status in our society, and are severely disadvantaged socially, vocationally, economically, and educationally;

(7) individuals with disabilities are a discrete and insular minority who have been faced with restrictions and limitations, subjected to a history of purposeful unequal treatment, and relegated to a position of political powerlessness in our society, based on characteristics that are beyond the control of such individuals and resulting from stereotypic assumptions not truly indicative of the individual ability of such individuals to participate in, and contribute to, society;

(8) the Nation's proper goals regarding individuals with disabilities are to assure equality of opportunity, full participation, independent living, and economic self-sufficiency for such individuals; and

(9) the continuing existence of unfair and unnecessary discrimination and prejudice denies people with disabilities the opportunity to compete on an equal basis and to pursue those opportunities for which our free society is justifiably famous, and costs the United States billions of dollars in unnecessary expenses resulting from dependency and non-productivity.

b) Purpose.—It is the purpose of this Act—

(1) to provide a clear and comprehensive national mandate for the elimination of discrimination against individuals with disabilities;

(2) to provide clear, strong, consistent, enforceable standards addressing discrimination against individuals with disabilities;

(3) to ensure that the Federal Government plays a central role in enforcing the standards established in this chapter on behalf of individuals with disabilities; and

(4) to invoke the sweep of congressional authority, including the power to enforce the fourteenth amendment and to regulate commerce, in order to address the major areas of discrimination faced day-to-day by people with disabilities.

It is interesting to note that eleven years later we are still dealing with just what the ADA really means. As you'll see when I discuss recent Supreme Court rulings, interpretation of the law rests with the Supreme Court, not with the words or the (apparent) intent of Congress when the law was passed. However, on the face of it, the

ADA is supposed to keep employers from not hiring you if you have a disability or from firing you if you develop or reveal a disability while you are employed. In addition, employers must make "reasonable accommodations" if you are otherwise qualified to perform the duties of the job, as long as it does not present an "undue hardship."

The ADA requires nondiscrimination in all employment practices on the basis of disability, and specific actions to ensure equal employment opportunity. Under the ADA, an employer may not discriminate against a person with a disability when the person is qualified to perform the essential functions of the job, with or without a reasonable accommodation.

The following list contains the definition of disability that appears in the ADA, and it is the same as the definition in the federal Rehabilitation Act of 1973, as amended. Definitions of disability from other government sources are also shown for comparison. There are many individuals who may meet the criteria for one or more of these definitions, but who do not see themselves as disabled.

Government Definitions of Disability

Americans with Disabilities Act

Definition of disability: a) a physical or mental impairment that substantially limits one or more of the major life activities of such individual; b) a record of such an impairment; or c) being regarded as having such an impairment.

U.S. Census Bureau, Using the Survey of Income and Program Participation (SIPP)

A person is considered to have a disability if he or she has difficulty performing certain functions (seeing, hearing, talking, walking, climbing stairs, and lifting and carrying), or has difficulty performing activities of daily living, or has difficulty with certain social roles (the school work for children, working at a job and around the house for adults). A person who is unable to perform one or more activities, or who uses an assistive device to get around, or who needs assistance from another person to perform basic activities is considered to have severe disability.

The National Health Interview (NHIS)

The traditional measure of disability employed by the NHIS is based on questions about limitations in one's major activity due to a *chronic health condition.*

(continued on page 70)

For those 18 to 64, the major activity is defined as working at a job or business.

The Current Population Survey (CPS)
Asks people whether they have a *work disability* (a condition that limits the kind or amount of work they can do) or a *severe work disability* (a condition that prevents them from working).

The Social Security Administration
For all individuals applying for disability benefits under title II, and for adults applying under title XVI, the definition of disability is the same. The law defines disability as the inability to engage in any substantial gainful activity by reason of any medically determinable physical or mental impairment(s) that can be expected to result in death or that has lasted or can be expected to last for a continuous period of not less than twelve months.

CIs often wax and wane in their symptoms; in other words, symptoms are worse on some days than on others. Many times chronic illnesses are invisible. The person may not have an obvious health problem, such as vision or hearing loss or the need for assistance in getting around by means of a cane, crutches, or a wheelchair. Examples could be those people with any of the following illnesses: cardiovascular diseases, such as congestive heart failure, atherosclerosis, or hypertension; lung or respiratory conditions, including asthma and lung cancer; diabetes; and some of the more recently recognized "silent" diseases such as fibromyalgia or chronic fatigue syndrome.

It must be remembered that in order for the ADA to be involved, the CI must result in a disability as defined by that law. There are many disability insurance programs that do not define disability as the ADA does, and even the Social Security Administration does not rely on that broad definition. This may be confusing, but it is important to remember, especially when invoking the ADA and "reasonable accommodations."

According to the ADA, major life activities are defined as, but not limited to:

- Seeing

- Learning

- Hearing

- Breathing
- Walking
- Working
- Caring for oneself

Physical or mental disability is defined as, but not limited to:

- Physiological disorder or condition, cosmetic disfigurement, or anatomical loss
- Mental or psychological disorder, such as mental retardation, emotional or mental illness, specific learning disabilities

These conditions may include:

- Cerebral palsy
- Epilepsy
- Muscular dystrophy
- Multiple sclerosis
- AIDS
- Cancer
- Heart disease
- Diabetes

The conditions recognized by the ADA as disabilities do *not* include:

- Minor or temporary disabilities
- Simple physical characteristics such as hair or eye color
- Environmental or cultural disadvantages
- Current illegal use of drugs
- Transvestitism
- Homosexuality
- Sexual behavior disorders
- Compulsive gambling
- Kleptomania
- Pyromania

The following are some important definitions as they appear in the ADA:

(8) Qualified individual with a disability.—The term "qualified individual with a disability" means an individual with a disability who, with or without reasonable accommodation, can perform the essential functions of the employment position that such individual holds or desires. For the purposes of this sub-chapter, consideration shall be given to the employer's judgment as to what functions of a job are essential, and if an employer has prepared a written description before advertising or interviewing applicants for the job, this description shall be considered evidence of the essential functions of the job.

(9) Reasonable accommodation.—The term "reasonable accommodation" may include—

(A) making existing facilities used by employees readily accessible to and usable by individuals with disabilities; and

(B) job restructuring, part-time or modified work schedules, reassignment to a vacant position, acquisition or modification of equipment or devices, appropriate adjustment or modifications of examinations, training materials or policies, the provision of qualified readers or interpreters, and other similar accommodations for individuals with disabilities.

(10) Undue hardship.—

(A) In general.—The term "undue hardship" means an action requiring significant difficulty or expense, when considered in light of the factors set forth in subparagraph (B).

(B) Factors to be considered.—In determining whether an accommodation would impose an undue hardship on a covered entity, factors to be considered include—

(i) the nature and cost of the accommodation needed under this Act;

(ii) the overall financial resources of the facility or facilities involved in the provision of the reasonable accommodation; the number of persons employed at such facility; the effect on expenses and resources, or the impact otherwise of such accommodation upon the operation of the facility;

(iii) the overall financial resources of the covered entity; the overall size of the business of a covered entity with respect to the number of its employees; the number, type, and location of its facilities;

(iv) the type of operation or operations of the covered entity, including the composition, structure, and functions of the workforce of such entity; the geographic separateness, administrative, or fiscal relationship of the facility or facilities in question to the covered entity.

I have deliberately included the actual text from the law because I want you to see just how the law is written. I could summarize it, but if I used the wrong word in that summary, and you then counted on what I wrote, you might be operating under a false assumption. Summaries are available and are posted on a number of government sites. The reality is that the Supreme Court is the only entity that knows how the law will be interpreted and enforced. Until it rules differently, the law stands as it appears above.

Who enforces the ADA? Where does a person go if he feels he has been discriminated against? The U.S. Equal Employment Opportunity Commission handles complaints regarding discrimination. Information on how to contact it is included in Appendix A.

The ADA is supposed to protect your rights to employment without discrimination, among other things. It was passed in 1990. How good a job has it done? In 2000, the U.S. Department of Justice issued a ten-year review. The report touched only briefly on employment issues. But among its overall efforts to increase awareness of the ADA, the Department of Justice reported that its activities included:

- Published more than forty technical assistance publications and disseminated several million copies, including technical assistance manuals, an ADA Guide for Small Businesses, an ADA Guide for Small Towns, a Guide to Disability Rights Laws, and a series of question-and-answer publications on a wide variety of issues;

- Provided $12 million to trade associations, disability rights groups, and other organizations to develop and disseminate 130 guides and fact sheets and twenty educational videotapes aimed at educating hotels and motels, grocery stores, restaurants, retail stores, dry cleaners, travel agents, medical professionals, child care providers, small businesses and other service providers, builders and contractors, town and city officials, courts, law enforcement, emergency response centers, people with disabilities, and other groups that are affected by the ADA;

- Placed a collection of ninety-four ADA publications developed by the Department, its grantees, and other federal agencies in 15,000 local public libraries, and sent a selection of thirty-three publications to 6,000 Chambers of Commerce around the country;

- Each year for the past seven years, notified 6 million businesses through IRS mailings of their ADA responsibilities and how to obtain information about specific ADA concerns or issues;

- Conducted training seminars, answered questions, disseminated information, and promoted awareness of the ADA nationwide at over 1,000 meetings of minority, disability, and professional organizations, and trade organizations representing business and government; and

- Reviewed hundreds of ADA publications, scripts, and videos developed by other agencies, grantees, and Disability and Business Technical Assistance Centers to ensure their legal and technical accuracy.[5]

Just as there are myths circulating relating to people with disabilities, there are also myths about the Americans with Disabilities Act. Below is a fact sheet produced in 1996 by the Department of Labor.

Dispelling Myths About the Americans with Disabilities Act[6]

Assumption: ADA suits are flooding the courts.

Fact: The ADA has resulted in a surprisingly small number of lawsuits—only about 650 nationwide in five years. That's tiny compared to the 6 million businesses; 666,000 public and private employers; and 80,000 units of state and local government that must comply.

Assumption: The ADA's definition of disability is broad and vague and has resulted in "bizarre and arcane" discrimination claims that are wasting the time of the EEOC and the courts.

Fact: As with any new statute, there is a period during which employers and employees learn about their rights and obligations under the law. While individuals have the right to file charges, not all charges are meritorious. The job of the EEOC investigator is to separate the wheat from the chaff. Further, the flexibility provided by the ADA definition of "disability" means that there will be individuals who bring claims for conditions that do not satisfy the statutory standards, and the claim will be dismissed.

Assumption: The ADA forces business and government to spend lots of money hiring unqualified people with disabilities.

Fact: To be protected by the ADA an individual must be qualified. No unqualified job applicant or employee with a disability can claim employment discrimination under the ADA. Employees or job applicants must meet all the requirements of the job and perform the essential functions of the job with or without reasonable accommodation. No accommodation must be provided if it would result in an undue hardship on the employer.

Assumption: The ADA, along with other laws such as the FMLA (Family Medical Leave Act) and Workers' Compensation, are squeezing out small businesses that cannot afford to hire human resource specialists to advise them regarding the complexities of these laws.

Fact: Truly small businesses, those with fewer than 15 employees, are not covered by the ADA. (The FMLA only applies to employers with 50 or more employees.) For employers who are covered, the ADA provides an undue hardship defense for reasonable accommodations that are unduly costly or burdensome. Smaller employers can more easily establish undue hardship because they have fewer resources.

Assumption: The ADA is being misused by people alleging mental and neurological impairments.

Fact: The ADA covers individuals with physical or mental impairments that substantially limit major life activities because individuals with such impairments have traditionally been subjected to pervasive employment discrimination. Just as the ADA excludes people with temporary physical problems, so does it exclude people with mild or short-term mental health problems. Neurological impairments are conditions or diseases involving the nervous system, including the brain, spinal cord, ganglia, nerves, and nerve centers. ADA charges indicate that there is significant discrimination against persons with neurological impairments. Psychiatric impairments involve a biological, social or psychological dysfunction. Individuals with psychiatric disabilities have traditionally been subjected to discrimination, not because they are unable to successfully perform job duties, but because of myths, fears and stereotypes associated with such impairments.

Assumption: The ADA is rigid and requires businesses to spend lots of money to make their existing facilities accessible.

Fact: The ADA is based on common sense. The law recognizes that altering existing structures is more costly than making new construction accessible. The law only requires that public accommodations (e.g., stores, banks, hotels, and restaurants) remove architectural barriers in existing facilities when it is "readily achievable", i.e., it can be done "without much difficulty or expense." Inexpensive, easy steps that can be taken include ramping one step; installing a bathroom grab bar; lowering a paper towel dispenser; rearranging furniture; installing offset hinges to widen a doorway; or painting new lines to create an accessible parking space.

Assumption: ADA requires that sign language interpreters be used in all situations involving persons who are deaf.

Fact: The ADA only requires that effective communication not exclude people with disabilities—which in many situations means providing written materials or exchanging notes. The law does not require any measure that would cause an undue financial or administrative burden.

Assumption: The ADA requires extensive renovation of all state and local government buildings to make them accessible.

Fact: The ADA requires all government programs, not all government buildings, to be accessible. "Program accessibility" is a very flexible requirement and does not require a local government to do anything that would result in an undue financial or administrative burden. Local governments have been subject to this requirement for many years under the Rehabilitation Act of 1973. Not every building, nor each part of every building needs to be accessible. Structural modifications are required only when there is no alternative available for providing program access. Let's say a town library has an inaccessible second floor. No elevator is needed if it provides "program accessibility" for persons using wheelchairs by having staff retrieve books.

Assumption: Everyone claims to be covered under the ADA.

Fact: To be protected under the law, a person must have an impairment that substantially limits a major life activity, must have a record of such an impairment, or must be regarded as having such an impairment. While people have the right to file charges, not all charges are meritorious. EEOC investigators are instructed to analyze whether a charging party has an ADA-protected disability. If an individual does not have a substantially limiting impairment (and does not allege "record of" or "regarded as" discrimination), the complaint is dismissed.

This information in this fact sheet came from the following sources: The U.S. Equal Employment Opportunity Commission and the U.S. Justice Department. July 1996.

What Progress Has Been Made?

The Department of Labor's Office of Disability Employment Policy included on its Web site the results of several surveys conducted from 1994 through 1995 about business' attitude toward the ADA. In general, the response was favorable, showing increased numbers of individuals with disabilities being hired and many industries believing that the ADA had had a positive impact on their industries.

However, a 1998 National Organization on Disability (N.O.D.)/ Harris Survey of Americans with Disabilities showed that although progress has been made, there are still some significant gaps in "securing jobs, education, accessible public transportation and in many areas of daily life including recreation and worship." Only 29 percent of those with disabilities ages 18 to 64 worked full- or part-time, while those with no disabilities had a 79 percent employment rate. Seventy-two percent of those with disabilities who were of working age said they "would prefer to work."

In a preliminary report excerpted from the N.O.D./Harris 2000 Survey of Americans with Disabilities on the N.O.D. Web site (www.nod.org), the figures had risen to 32 percent employment for those with disabilities and 81 percent for those without disabilities. This was despite almost full employment in a strong economy. There were some encouraging signs, however. When those individuals with severe disabilities who said they were unable to work were removed from the employment calculation, the employment rate for those with disabilities rose to 56 percent. And when only those between the ages of 18 and 29 were counted, a significant fact appeared. The gap between people with and without disabilities was only 25 percentage points, smaller than any other age group. This younger age group usually has fewer and less severe disabilities, but they are also an age group that has benefited from the inclusive efforts of the ADA at their entry point into their careers.

Discrimination has not been eliminated yet. The 2000 Harris study showed that more than three out of ten people say they have been discriminated against in the workplace. Most often that discrimination comes in the form of not being hired for a job in the first place.

Supreme Court Cases and the ADA

In the eleven years since the ADA was passed, individuals with disabilities are not seeing the improvements in employment opportunities that were anticipated. The Equal Employment Opportunity Commission (EEOC) is the branch of the government charged with enforcing the ADA. The results of the actions taken by the EEOC have been mixed. According to a report on the Department of Labor's Office of Disability Employment Policy, many of the court cases have dealt with substantial limitation, disability definition, and reasonable accommodation.

Issues

A number of issues have been raised in court cases on the questions of what a disability is and whether an individual with a disability is "qualified." Issues have been raised around the provision that requires a disability to substantially limit a major life activity, and the provision that requires employees with such disabilities to perform the essential function of the job, despite the disabilities.

- Issues stemming from whether a person is "qualified" are (1) "What are the essential functions of the job?" and (2) "Can the individual perform the essential functions of the job with or without reasonable accommodations?"

- Courts are ruling on the "substantial limitation" concept by determining when symptoms are severe enough to meet this requirement. This issue impacts people with cancer, psychiatric disabilities, multiple sclerosis, and other disabilities that have episodic symptoms.

Court Findings

Several courts have found that there are no "per se" disabilities, although the EEOC's position states that "certain impairments such as HIV, by their nature may be disabling." Many times the courts have ruled that in order to be considered substantially limited in working, plaintiffs must be unable to perform across a class of related jobs, not just be unable to perform in one particular position or situation. The burden is upon the individual to prove that her disability is substantial and yet that she is able to perform the job she is applying for.

One area in which the EEOC has had to change its stance has been "mitigating measures." "Mitigating measures" refers to the effect that medication, corrective lenses, and other medical devices or treatment will have upon a condition. The Supreme Court held in *Sutton v. United Air Lines* and *Murphy v. United Parcel Service* that these measures should be taken into consideration in determining whether a disability does exist.

The Sutton case dealt with two sisters with near-sightedness that was correctable with lenses. They had applied to United Airlines for commercial airline pilots' positions. When they were turned down, they filed with the EEOC. The Murphy case dealt with a United Parcel Service mechanic with high blood pressure. With medication, the blood pressure was under control, but he could not obtain a commercial operator's license, which he needed in order to operate the commercial motor vehicles. In both cases, the Supreme Court determined that a disability did not exist.

At the same time, the court did note that medication could have a negative effect that should be considered in determining the substantial limitation. It also decided that even with some "mitigating measures," such as a wheelchair, a person could still be substantially limited. A perception by employers that the individual had a substantially limited impairment could still be covered under the ADA, in the case of stereotyping.

According to an article in *HR Magazine*, the EEOC reported that disability-related complaints have averaged more than 20 percent of all job discrimination complaints since 1994. However, approximately 50 percent of them are dismissed by the EEOC as having "no reasonable cause."[7]

Even when the cases do move to court, the employers are winning more than 95 percent of them, according to an American Bar Association report. One interesting fact is that the majority of the cases filed deal with termination of an employee, *not* with any hiring situations. Since one of the primary motivations behind the ADA was to improve the employment of those with disabilities, this would indicate that the law is not having the desired effect.

In fact, many advocates look to the statistics that have been gathered to date and say there has been no real improvement. The statistics actually show that there was a decline of eight points in the employment of white males with disabilities. However, those studies that have been done do not take into consideration either the changing economy or job retention.

There is much anecdotal information being released that seems to indicate that the ADA has had a positive impact on job employment for those with disabilities. However, at this point, there are not enough statistics to prove that. Although the Supreme Court ruled in favor of a professional golfer in his request to use a golf cart in the PGA (Casey Martin) because he has a health condition that causes fatigue, it ruled against two Alabama state employees who sought the right to sue Alabama for discrimination. In February 2001, the Supreme Court ruled that "because there is 'no pattern of unconstitutional discrimination' by the state" the individuals did not have the right to sue for damages. The decision was a five to four vote that reversed a federal appeals court decision that had sided with the state employees.

Disability advocates voiced their disappointment in the decision. N.O.D. President Alan A. Reich said, "It is a shame that this decision, reflecting the Court's support for state's rights, overrides people's rights. The Americans with Disabilities Act is a decade-old legal protection of the rights of America's 54 million citizens who have disabilities. Because anybody can join the disability community in an instant, all people are threatened by any amendment that weakens the A.D.A."[8]

In January 2002, the Supreme Court ruled against Ella Williams in her suit against Toyota, saying that her carpal tunnel syndrome did not qualify her for special treatment on the job. The unanimous

Supreme Court ruling went against the federal appeals court, which had found she was disabled under the ADA. In response to the decision, Reich made the following statement: "Congress intended that the ADA protect persons who have impairments that substantially limit them from performing one or more major life activities. The implication in the Court's written opinion that work is not a major life activity is inimical to the intent of this law and to people with disabilities. We want to be wage earners, support our families and contribute to America like everyone else."[9]

Carpal tunnel syndrome and other repetitive stress injuries have become a major problem for many workers. With this ruling, I believe that there will be many more individuals who will face major problems in continuing with the jobs that caused their injuries or in finding new ones. I feel that the decision in *Toyota v. Williams* is one that takes workers a step backward in trying to achieve employment and an improved quality of life. As we move into the twenty-first century and the second decade of existence for the Americans with Disabilities Act, it is still unclear just how effective this law will ultimately be in obtaining equal opportunities for employment for individuals with disabilities.

Notes

1. Disability Statistic Center, "The Employment of Persons with Limitations in Physical Functioning, 2000." www.dsc.ucsf.edu.

2. The complete text of the New Freedom Initiative is available at http://wdsc.doleta.gov/disability/htmldocs/new_freedom.html.

3. U.S. Health and Human Services Department. www.hhs.gov/newfreedom/init.htm.

4. The complete bill is available on the U.S. Department of Justice disability rights Web site (www.usdoj.gov/crt/ada/adahom1.htm) and on the U.S. Equal Opportunity Employment Commission's Web site (www.eeoc.gov/laws/ada.html).

5. U.S. Department of Justice, Civil Rights Division, Disability Rights Section, "Enforcing the ADA: Looking Back on a Decade of Progress—A Special Tenth Anniversary Report, June, 2000." www.usdoj.gov/crt/ada/pubs/10thrpt.htm.

6. U.S. Department of Labor, Office of Disability Employment Policy Publications Fact Sheet, "Dispelling Myths About the Americans with Disabilities Act," July 1996. www.dol.gov/dol/odep/public/media/reports/ek96/lawmyth.htm.

82 I'd Rather Be Working

7. Susan J. Wells, "Is the ADA Working?" *HR Magazine,* April 2001.

8. National Organization on Disability, "National Organization on Disability Surprised, Disappointed by Supreme Court Decision," press release, February 21, 2001. www.nod.org.

9. National Organization on Disability, "Supreme Court Decision in Toyota v. Williams Raises Concern for the Americans with Disabilities Act (ADA)," press release, January 10, 2002. www.nod.org.

Five

U.S. Department of Labor: Helping You Find Work

The Department of Labor (DOL) has a tremendous amount of information available both on its multiple Web sites and in print for anyone seeking work, whether he or she has disabilities or not. The DOL's mission is to address the needs of America's workforce through a number of offices within the department and in cooperation with state and local governments as well as private for-profit businesses and nonprofit organizations. The department's Web site has been upgraded to be more user-friendly, with improved access to information and services and a guaranteed rapid response to e-mail inquiries from both employees and employers.

One-Stop Career Centers

Perhaps the biggest change at the Department of Labor and across the United States is in what used to be called state employment agencies, where individuals go to file for unemployment benefits (if they are eligible), and to find a job. However, in response to requests from both employees and employers, such agencies are now "One-Stop Career Centers" that connect employment, education, and training services into a coherent network of resources at the local, state, and national level. This new system links the nation's employers to a variety of qualified applicants and provides job seekers with access to employment and training opportunities next door and across the country. The following is the Department of Labor's description of the centers.

> Strong alliances at the point of service delivery are essential—employment service, education and training agencies, unemployment insurance, vocational education agencies, vocational rehabilitation agencies, community colleges, and both nonprofit

and for-profit organizations are united to furnish the customers with unified service. These partners are also making sure the system fully serves the disabled community.

Innovation and partnership have also led to the transformation of traditional Job Service and Job Training Partnership Act (JTPA) offices into One-Stop Career Centers. In many areas, community colleges and public libraries may also serve as convenient access points for the public. Customers can visit the Centers in person or directly connect to the Center's information holdings through personal computers or kiosk remote access. For many, an Internet browser is all that's needed.

While individual state systems may reflect a range of titles—"No Wrong Door," "Workforce Development," "Our State 'Works!'"—all are affiliated with America's One-Stop Career Center System. The partners in Center service teams may also vary from state to state, but the following services are available.

One-Stop Services for Individuals:

- Information about local, state and national labor markets
- Job and career resource room (computers, faxes, telephones)
- Job listings
- Hiring requirements
- Job referral and placement and quality of education and training programs
- Initial screening for training eligibility
- Testing and assessment
- Job search skills
- Assistance in filing unemployment insurance claims

One-Stop Services available for Employers are:

- Recruitment and pre-screening of qualified applicants
- Easy access to post job listings on America's Job Bank (AJB)
- Job and industry growth trends and forecasts
- Wage data and other valuable labor market information
- Compliance information on federal legislation, e.g., Americans with Disabilities Act

Many of the services for individuals also are applicable for those with disabilities, and so will be helpful for them as well as allowing access to vocational rehabilitation. Check the U.S. website http:// usworkforce.org/onestop/index.htm for more information and a link to your state's One-Stop Centers.[1]

Office of Disability Employment Policy

Within the Department of Labor is the Office of Disability Employment Policy (ODEP) (www.dol.gov/dol/odep.htm). The mission of the ODEP, under the leadership of an assistant secretary, is to bring a heightened and permanent long-term focus to the goal of increasing employment of persons with disabilities. This will be achieved through policy analysis, technical assistance, and development of best practices, as well as outreach, education, constituent services, and promoting ODEP's mission among employers.

In announcing the president's FY 2002 budget, which proposed an additional $20.3 million and ten new full-time positions for the office, Secretary Elaine L. Chao stated, "It is not only important to give people with disabilities training and access to assistive technology—but also the ability to become more active citizens in their communities."[2] At this writing, the FY 2002 budget has not been approved yet, so be sure to check the ODEP Web site for the current situation when you read this book.

Although much of the material in the new list of programs for the ODEP focuses on employers, there is still a great deal of information for individuals with disabilities, whether they are currently employed or are seeking work. The programs in place in FY 2001 include those described in the following sections, among others.

Cultural Diversity Initiative

The Cultural Diversity Initiative addresses the high numbers of minorities with disabilities who are unemployed. The U.S. Census Bureau's 1994–1995 data showed that 72.2 percent of African Americans with disabilities and 51.9 percent of Hispanics with disabilities were not working. Those in both groups with severe disabilities have an even higher level of unemployment.

People with disabilities from culturally diverse backgrounds experience twice the discrimination experienced by nondisabled people in the minority community. Both disability and race complicate the situation. Other problems that minorities with disabilities face include limited access to rehabilitation services and educational opportunities, inadequate transportation and housing in disadvantaged communities, and lack of mentors and role models in the workplace. The DOL also found that both mainstream and minority communities and religious organizations tend to overlook their capability to support the employment of minority individuals with disabilities, and that cultural differences are not clearly understood by individuals or organizations designing programs to support the employment of minority persons with disabilities.

The DOL and ODEP are working with minority organizations to bring about changes in the situation. They feel that it will take the efforts of many organizations and employers to reverse the negative employment picture for minorities with disabilities.

Employment Assistance Referral Network

The Employment Assistance Referral Network (EARN) is a new service that provides all employers with a direct connection to their local community service providers. EARN, a national toll-free service, makes it simple for all businesses to locate applicants with disabilities for any type of position. When EARN receives a call from an employer who wants to recruit qualified candidates with disabilities, the EARN staff takes the employer's job vacancy information and then checks with local employment providers to find those who have job candidates with the appropriate qualifications.

Once these providers are identified, EARN calls the employer back. The employer receives the information on the provider and can then approach that organization to set up a meeting. This procedure gives the employer complete control of how and when contact is made with that employment provider and then the potential job applicant.

EARN also provides employers with technical assistance related to the employment of people with disabilities, such as tax credits, disability-related laws, lawful job-interviewing techniques, recruitment and hiring strategies, ways of dealing with coworker attitudes, personal assistance services, and reasonable accommodations.

EARN operates Monday through Friday, from 9:00 A.M. to 10:00 P.M. EST. Contact is 866-EarnNow (866-327-6669); www. earnworks.com.

Veterans Employment and Training Service

The Department of Labor's Veterans' Employment and Training Service, through cooperative efforts with, and grants to, each state, offers employment and training services to eligible veterans through two principal programs:

- Disabled Veterans' Outreach Program

- Local Veterans' Employment Representatives Program

Disabled Veterans' Outreach Program (DVOP) specialists develop job and training opportunities for veterans, with special emphasis on veterans with service-connected disabilities. DVOP specialists provide direct services to veterans enabling them to be competitive in the labor market. They provide outreach and offer assistance to disabled and other veterans by promoting community and employer support for employment and training opportunities, including apprenticeship and on-the-job training.

DVOP specialists work with employers, veterans' organizations, the Departments of Veterans Affairs and Defense, and community-based organizations to link veterans with appropriate jobs and training opportunities. DVOP specialists serve as case managers for veterans enrolled in federally funded job training programs such as the Department of Veterans Affairs' Vocational Rehabilitation Program, and other veterans with serious disadvantages in the job market. DVOP specialists are available to those veterans and their employers to help ensure that necessary follow-up services are provided to promote job retention.

The U.S. Department of Labor provides grant funds to each state's employment service to maintain DVOP specialist positions in the state. The staffing formula and current appropriations level support about 1,400 DVOP specialists nationally. DVOP specialists are employees of the state and are generally located in state employment service offices. About one-quarter of the specialists are stationed full- or part-time in locations other than employment service offices.

DVOP specialists may be stationed at regional offices and medical or veterans' outreach centers of the Department of Veterans Affairs, state or county veterans' service offices, Job Training Partnership Act program offices, community-based organizations, and military installations. To contact a DVOP specialist, call or visit the nearest "One-Stop Career Center" (sometimes known as state workforce or employment) agency listed in the state government section of your phone book.

Technical Assistance Materials

Technical Assistance Materials providing valuable information for employers and workers with disabilities are available in fact sheets, ADA brochures, reports, and other publications.

The fact sheets cover such topics for employees as:

- Accommodations
- Affirmative action
- Alternative dispute resolution or mediation
- Attitudinal barriers
- Career development for persons with disabilities
- Cost and benefits of accommodations
- Essential elements of an effective job search
- Facts about the Americans with Disabilities Act
- Interviewing tips for the job applicant
- Job accommodations that come in groups of one
- Self-employment profiles
- Small business and self-employment for people with disabilities
- Ticket to Work and Work Incentive Improvement Act
- What to do if you have been discriminated against

Most of these are available in print or can be downloaded from the Office of Disability Employment Web site (www.dol.gov/dol/odep/public/programs.program.htm).

Women's Bureau

The Department of Labor's Women's Bureau "champions the concerns of working women through the leadership of its director, deputy director, and the efforts of a dedicated national and regional staff." The Women's Bureau's mandate states: "It shall be the duty of said bureau to formulate standards and policies which shall promote the welfare of wage-earning women, improve their working conditions, increase their efficiency, and advance their opportunities for profitable employment."

However, other than having one pamphlet that covers women and disability discrimination, there really isn't that much for women with disabilities at this site unless they just happen to be women veterans of the U.S. military forces and are disabled.

Bureau of Labor Statistics

One of the most comprehensive units within the DOL is the Bureau of Labor Statistics. The Bureau of Labor Statistics provides the government and public with information on the latest unemployment figures as well as identifies the areas of the workforce that are expected to change over the next few years.

Occupational Outlook Handbook

An excellent place to begin your specific job research is online at the Bureau of Labor Statistics Occupational Outlook Web site, www/bls.gov/oco/home.htm. The *Occupational Outlook Handbook* is a nationally recognized source of career information, designed to provide valuable assistance to individuals making decisions about their future work lives. Revised every two years, the handbook describes the characteristics of a wide range of occupations: what workers in those areas actually do, typical working conditions, training and education needed, earnings, and expected job prospects.

Career Guide to Industries

The *Career Guide to Industries*, on the Web at http://stats.bls.gov/oco/cg/home.htm provides information on available careers by industry, including the nature of the industry, working conditions, employment, occupations in the industry, training and advancement, earnings and benefits, employment outlook, and lists of organizations that can provide additional information. The 2000–2001 edition of the career guide discusses over forty-two industries, accounting for over seven out of every ten wage and salary jobs in 1998. This information is given from an occupational perspective.

Although you may not think you would be interested in the figures and tables of statistical information provided on this site and in the print editions (which can usually be found at your local public library), the career guide can help give you an idea of which jobs are expected to be increasing in the coming years and which ones may be decreasing.

Employment Projections

Employment growth or decline is measured two ways: numeric and percent change. Numeric change is the actual number of jobs gained or lost over the period the projection is covering. Percent change is the rate of employment growth or decline during the period.

For example, between 2000 and 2010, employment of child-care workers is expected to change from 1,192,578 to 1,319,338—an increase of nearly 127,000 jobs. Employment of speech-language pathologists is expected to grow from 87,931 to 122,398—an increase of more than 34,000 jobs. In numeric terms, as Figure 5.1 shows, this means that four times as many new jobs are projected for child-care workers as for speech-language pathologists between 2000 and 2010. Percent change tells a different story. As Figure 5.2 shows, employment of speech-language pathologists is expected to grow nearly four times as fast as that of child-care workers.

Projected Top Industries

Health services, business services, social services, and engineering, management, and related services are expected to account for almost

Figure 5.1. Employment growth (thousands) in selected occupations, projected 2000–2010.[3]

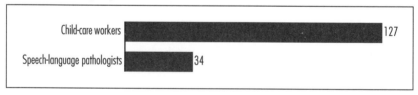

Figure 5.2. Employment growth (percent) in selected occupations, projected 2000–2010.[4]

one of every two nonfarm wage and salary jobs added to the economy through 2008. Professional specialty occupations are projected to increase the fastest and to add the most jobs—5.3 million. Service workers are expected to add 3.9 million jobs. These two groups—on opposite ends of the educational attainment and earnings spectrum—are expected to provide 45 percent of the total projected job growth over the ten-year period.

Other occupations that are also expected to see growth are executive, administrative, and managerial; technicians and related support; and marketing and sales. Administrative support occupations, including clerical, are projected to grow slower than the average, reflecting the impact of office automation.

Precision production, craft, and repair occupations and operators, fabricators, and laborers are projected to grow much more slowly than the average due to continuing advances in technology, changes in production methods, and the overall decline in manufacturing employment.

Fastest-Growing Occupations

The ten fastest growing occupations as projected for 2000–2020 by the Bureau of Labor Statistics' latest release[5] will be:

Computer software engineers—applications 100%

Computer support specialists 97%

Computer software engineers, systems software 90%

Network and computer systems administrators 82%

Network systems and data communications analysts . . . 77%

Desktop publishers 67%

Database administrators 66%

Personal and home care aides 62%

Computer systems analysts 60%

Medical assistants 57%

Job Growth

According to the same release,[6] the ten occupations with the largest job growth will be:

Combined food preparation and
serving workers, including fast food . . . . 673,000 jobs (30%)

Customer service representatives . . . . . . 631,000 jobs (32%)

Registered nurses . . . . 561,000 jobs (26%)

Retail salespersons . . . . 510,000 jobs (12%)

Computer support specialists . . . . 490,000 jobs (97%)

Cashiers, except gaming . . . . 474,000 jobs (14%)

Office clerks, general . . . . 430,000 jobs (16%)

Security guards . . . . 391,000 jobs (35%)

Computer software
engineers—applications . . . . 380,000 jobs (100%)

Waiters and waitresses . . . . 364,000 jobs (18%)

Wage and Salary Growth

Computer and data-processing services (117 percent) are projected
to lead the ten industries with the fastest wage and salary employment growth for the 1998–2008 period. The others in the top ten
are health services, not elsewhere classified (67 percent); residential
care (57 percent); management and public relations (45 percent);
personnel supply services (43 percent); miscellaneous equipment
rental and leasing (43 percent); museums, botanical and zoological
gardens (42 percent); and research and testing services, miscellaneous
transportation services, and security and commodity brokers, all with
40 percent expected growth.

Education and Training Requirements

The report also breaks the employment and total job openings down
by education and training. Employment in all education and training
categories that generally require an associate degree or more education is projected to grow faster than the 14 percent average for all
occupations. In contrast, all other categories are expected to grow
less than 14 percent.

What Do the Numbers Mean to You?

The meaning of these statistics to you is going to depend upon what
area of experience or interest you listed in your self-evaluation and

the goals you set for yourself in Chapter 3. By combining your interests and/or your experience and education with the limitations caused by your chronic illness, and then considering the projections given earlier, you can begin to develop a direction for your future work.

Let's look at a hypothetical situation. Lil has worked in the office of a large company for fifteen years in clerical positions. She has seen her job change as more and more of the office work has been converted to computers; most of the information she once spent the majority of her time filing in large metal file cabinets is now kept on computer disks and tapes. For the last two years, she has spent her eight-hour workday entering information into a computer. She's also developed repetitive stress syndrome, more commonly known as carpal tunnel syndrome. Despite treatment with nonsteroidal anti-inflammatory drugs, she ends every day in pain.

Lil must make some decisions soon. If she wants to continue with her present job, something will have to change. Her doctor is talking about surgery on her wrists, but there is no guarantee the pain won't come back. Lil is beginning to consider making a major job change because she doesn't like the idea of surgery.

In looking for information on the Internet, she finds her way to the Department of Labor and the *Occupational Outlook Handbook* and then to the *Career Guide to Industries*. Lil has already seen how much work in the office has been taken over by computers and the career guide tells her that her job field is going to grow slower than others in the coming ten years. Since she doesn't want to move into a supervisory position, it looks like she has few options with her present employer. Maybe it's time for a change to another job field or to another company. Knowing what the fastest-growing occupations and job fields over the next ten years are gives her a starting point for finding something she knows will be needed, and perhaps that occupation will be something for which she can train.

Occupational Outlook Quarterly

Another publication of the Bureau of Labor Statistics is the *Occupational Outlook Quarterly*, which provides more timely information on employment statistics than the *Occupational Outlook Handbook* and includes articles that cover various occupations and job fields. The *OOQ* is available both online (www.bls.gov/opub/ooq/ooqhome.htm) and in print at some libraries.

To give you an idea of the type of information provided in the

Occupational Outlook Quarterly, the article on computer support specialists that appeared in the spring 2001 issue follows at the end of this section. More can be found online at the Bureau of Labor Statistics site (www.bls/gov/oco/hom/htm).

Examples of articles published in recent issues of the *Occupational Outlook Quarterly* include the following:

- "You're a Genealogist"

- "Librarian"

- "The Changing Temporary Work Force"

- "Instructional Coordinators"

- "Financial Analysts and Personal Financial Advisors"

- "Paid Jobs in Charitable Nonprofits"

- "You're an Arborist"

Computer Support Specialists[7]

Almost every computer user encounters a problem occasionally, whether it's the disaster of a crashing hard drive or the annoyance of a forgotten password. Some people try to solve the problem on their own. Others seek the aid of workers trained to resolve technical emergencies, predicaments, and glitches. These workers are known as computer support specialists.

There were more than 400,000 computer support specialists working in the United States in 1998. According to the Bureau of Labor Statistics (BLS), the occupation is projected to be one of the fastest growing over the next decade—more than doubling in employment between 1998 and 2008.

These jobs will be filled by both newly trained and existing computer support specialists who continue to keep their skills current. This article describes what computer support specialists do, what their employment outlook is, how much they earn, and what training they need.

Nature of the Work

The explosion of computer use has created a high demand for computer support specialists to provide technical assistance, support, and advice to customers and other users. This group includes technical support specialists and help-desk technicians. These troubleshooters interpret problems and provide technical support for hardware, software, and systems. They answer phone calls, analyze problems using automated diagnostic programs, and resolve recurrent difficulties.

Support specialists may work either within a company or other organization or directly for a computer hardware or software vendor. Increasingly, these technical professionals give customer support as contractors for help desks or support services firms.

Technical Support Specialists. These troubleshooters assist an organization's computer users, many of whom are non-technical employees, when these users run into computer problems they cannot resolve on their own. Technical support specialists install, modify, clean, and repair computer hardware and software. They also may work on monitors, keyboards, printers, and mice.

Technical support specialists answer phone calls from their organization's computer users and may run automatic diagnostic programs to resolve problems. They may also write training manuals and teach computer users about new computer hardware and software. In addition, technical support specialists oversee the daily performance of their company's computer systems and evaluate software programs for usefulness.

Help-Desk Technicians. These workers assist computer users with the inevitable hardware and software questions not addressed in a product's instruction manual. Help-desk technicians field telephone calls and e-mail messages from customers seeking guidance on technical problems. In responding to these requests for guidance, technicians must listen carefully to the customer, ask questions to diagnose the nature of the problem, and then patiently walk the customer through the problem-solving steps.

Because help-desk technicians deal directly with customer issues, companies value them as a source of feedback on their products. Most computer support specialists start out as help-desk technicians.

Working Conditions

Computer support specialists normally work in well-lit, comfortable offices or computer laboratories. They usually work about forty hours a week, but that may include evening or weekend work if the employer requires computer support over extended hours. Overtime may be necessary when unexpected technical problems arise. Like other workers who type on a keyboard for long periods, computer support specialists are susceptible to eyestrain, back discomfort, and hand and wrist problems, such as carpal tunnel syndrome.

Computer support specialists interact with all types of computer users in answering questions and giving advice. Those who work as consultants are away from their offices much of the time, spending months working in a client's office.

As computer networks expand, more computer support specialists may be able to connect to a customer's computer remotely using modems, laptops, e-mail, and the Internet to provide technical support to computer users. In such cases, computer support specialists would reduce or eliminate travel to the customer's workplace.

Employment and Outlook

Computer support specialists held about 429,000 jobs in 1998. Although they worked in a wide range of industries, nearly one-third were in the business services industries, principally computer and data processing services. Other industries that employed substantial numbers of computer support specialists include banks, government agencies, insurance companies, educational institutions, personnel supply services, and wholesale and retail vendors of computers, office equipment, appliances and home electronic equipment. Many computer support specialists also worked for manufacturers of computers and other office equipment and for firms making electronic components and other accessories.

Employers of computer support specialists range from startup companies to established industry leaders. With the continued development of the Internet, telephony, e-mail, and other communications, industries not typically associated with computers—such as construction—need computer support specialists. Small and large firms across all industries are either expanding or developing computer systems, creating an immediate need for computer support specialists.

The occupation of computer support specialist is projected to be the second fastest growing occupation over the 1998–2008 decade. Employment is expected to increase much faster than average as technology becomes more sophisticated and organizations continue to adopt and integrate it. Growth will continue to be driven by rapid gains in computer and data processing services, which is projected to be the fastest growing industry in the U.S. economy.

The falling prices of computer hardware and software should help businesses expand their computing applications and integrate new technology into their operations. To maintain a competitive edge and operate more cost effectively, firms will continue to demand computer professionals who are both knowledgeable about the latest technology and able to apply this technology to meet the organization's needs.

Demand for computer support specialists also is expected to increase because of the rapid pace of improved technology. As computers and software become more complex, support specialists will be needed to provide technical assistance to customers and other users. Consulting opportunities for computer support specialists also should continue to grow as businesses increasingly need help managing, upgrading, and customizing more complex computer systems.

Qualifications, Training, and Advancement

People interested in becoming computer support specialists must have strong problem-solving, analytical, and communication skills because troubleshooting and helping others are a vital part of the job. The constant interaction with other computer personnel, customers, and employees requires computer support specialists to communicate effectively on paper, via e-mail, and in person. Strong writing skills are important for preparing manuals for employees and customers.

Because of the wide range of skills required, there are several ways to become a computer support specialist. Employers seek computer professionals who have fundamental computer skills and good interpersonal and communication skills. College graduates with computer-related bachelor's degrees should enjoy very favorable employment prospects, particularly if they have supplemented their formal education with relevant work experience. But because of the rapid growth in demand for computer support specialists, those who have strong computer skills who do not have a bachelor's degree should continue to qualify for some entry-level positions.

Many companies are becoming more flexible about requiring a college degree for support positions because of the rampant demand for specialists. However, certification and practical experience demonstrating the skills will be essential for applicants without a degree. Completion of a certification-training program, offered by a variety of vendors and product makers, may help some people to qualify for entry-level positions. Relevant computer experience may substitute for formal education.

Beginning computer support specialists usually start out dealing directly with customers or the in-house users. Then, they are often able to advance into more responsible positions in which they use what they learned from customers to improve the design and efficiency of future products. Job promotions usually depend more on performance than on possession of a degree. Eventually, some computer support specialists become programmers, designing products rather than assisting users. Computer support specialists at hardware and software companies often enjoy the rapid upward mobility; advancement sometimes comes within months of initial employment.

As technology continues to improve, computer support specialists must keep their skills current and acquire new ones. Many continuing education programs are offered by employers, hardware and software vendors, colleges and universities, and private training institutions. Additional training and skills enhancement may come from professional development seminars offered by professional computing services firms.

Sources of Additional Information

Your local library has information about computer support specialists and the computer industry. For additional information about a career as a computer support specialist, contact:

The Association of Computer Support Specialists
218 Huntington Road
Bridgeport, CT 06608
(203) 332-1524
http://www.acss.org

The Association of Support Professionals
66 Mount Auburn Street
Watertown, MA 02472
(617) 924-3944, extension 14
http://www.asponline.com

For information on training leading to vendor-sponsored certifications, contact vendors and product makers individually.

Notes

1. U.S. Department of Labor, "America's One-Stop Career System." www.usworkforce.org/onestop/index.htm.

2. U.S. Department of Labor, Office of Disability Employment Policy Fact Sheet, "About Us." www.dol.gov/dol/odep/public/about/about.htm.

3. U.S. Department of Labor, Bureau of Labor Statistics, "Charting the Projections: 2000–2010," *Occupational Outlook Quarterly* 45, 4 (2001–2002), p. 6, U.S. Department of Labor.

4. Ibid.

5. U.S. Department of Labor, Bureau of Labor Statistics, news release, December 3, 2001. www.bls.gov/news.release/ecopro.t06.htm.

6. U.S. Department of Labor, Bureau of Labor Statistics, news release, December 3, 2001. www.bls.gov/news.release/ecopro.t07.htm

7. Roger Moncarz, "Computer Support Specialists," *Occupational Outlook Quarterly,* Spring 2001. www.bls.gov/opub/ooq/2001/spring/contents.htm.

CHAPTER Six

Job Accommodation Network: Helping You Do Your Work

The Job Accommodation Network (JAN) has perhaps the most tangible impact on those wanting to keep their present job or to find new employment they can do. JAN is an international toll-free consulting service that provides free information and services about job accommodations and the employability of people with functional limitations.

JAN supplies information on relevant options concerning job accommodations to employers, rehabilitation professionals, and people with disabilities throughout the United States and overseas. The development of the JAN system has been achieved through the collaborative efforts of the U.S. Department of Labor—Office of Disability Employment Policy, the West Virginia Rehabilitation Research and Training Center at West Virginia University, Employment and Immigration Canada, and private industry throughout North America.

What Is the Job Accommodation Network?

JAN represents the most comprehensive resource for job accommodations currently available. Its work greatly enhances the ability of employers to provide reasonable and appropriate job accommodations for qualified persons with disabilities and increases job opportunities for persons with disabilities.[1]

What Is JAN?[2]

The mission of JAN is to assist in the hiring, retraining, retention or advancement of persons with disabilities by providing accommodation information. Anyone can contact JAN for information and be assured of the confidentiality of their call.

Who Uses JAN?

JAN's work helps:

Employers

1. hire, retain, and promote qualified employees with disabilities;
2. reduce worker's compensation and other insurance costs;
3. address issues pertaining to accessibility; and
4. provide accommodation options and practical solutions;

Rehabilitation Professionals

1. facilitate placement of clients through accommodation assistance;
2. discover resources for device fabrication and modification;

Persons with Disabilities

1. acquire accommodation information;
2. discover other organizations, support groups, government agencies, and placement agencies.

Anyone can call JAN for information or go to the Web site at www.jan.wvu.edu. There are almost one and a half million contacts on the Web site each year, and that doesn't count the approximately 40,000 telephone queries each year. Contacts are usually made by individuals with disabilities, or by family members, employers, or rehabilitation and education specialists.

Right after the ADA was passed, employers outnumbered individuals in making contact by telephone, but in recent years individuals account for the highest percentage of calls, while those from employers and rehabilitation and educational professionals have dropped. According to a congressional report made on July 26, 2000, employers are evidently now using the Internet more frequently than the telephone to make inquiries.

Recent trends in the contacts with JAN show that there are a rising number of contacts that deal with conflicts between employees and employers, primarily regarding failure to provide accommodation. Also, since the Supreme Court cases in 1999, calls regarding the definition of a disability have almost doubled.

The majority of contacts from employers currently have more to do with accommodation and retention of employees, with the calls about new hires dropping well below 10 percent of the overall calls.

In looking at the accommodations and experiences of the first decade of the ADA, the JAN report to Congress, which was given by Barbara T. Judy, who is project manager for JAN, listed the following suggestions [italics added for emphasis throughout this excerpt]:

- Improvements in technological equipment by *persons who understand the needs of persons with disabilities as well as the requirements of the workplace* must continue.

- Continued and enhanced efforts by the education system at all levels must occur if individuals with disabilities are to be prepared to enter the competitive workforce.

- Persons with disabilities *must put forth every effort to receive the skills and knowledge they will need to be successful workers at any level.*

- *The business community must continue to be informed about advances in technology that can be of assistance to them and to their employee population.*

- Finally, leaders in *federal and state government must endeavor to make sound decisions that encompass ALL of their constituents, including persons with disabilities.*[3]

What Is Accommodation?

To give you a better idea of what accommodation is and is not, let's look at some questions and answers on accommodation, as prepared by the U.S. Equal Employment Opportunity Commission. Then we will look at the description of the job accommodation process, as stated by JAN.

Some Questions on Accommodation[4]

Q. What is "reasonable accommodation?"

A. Reasonable accommodation is any modification or adjustment to a job or the work environment that will enable a qualified applicant or employee with a disability to participate in the application process or to perform essential job functions. Reasonable accommodation also includes adjustments to assure that a qualified individual with a disability has rights and privileges in employment equal to those of employees without disabilities.

Q. What are some of the accommodations applicants and employees may need?

A. Examples of reasonable accommodation include making existing facilities used by employees readily accessible to and usable by an individual with a disability; restructuring a job; modifying work schedules; acquiring or modifying equipment; providing qualified readers or interpreters; or appropriately modifying examinations, training, or other programs.

Reasonable accommodation also may include reassigning a current employee to a vacant position for which the individual is qualified, if the person is unable to do the original job because of a disability even with an accommodation. However, there is no obligation to find a position for an applicant who is not qualified for the position sought. Employers are not required to lower quality or quantity standards as an accommodation; nor are they obligated to provide personal use items such as glasses or hearing aids.

The decision as to the appropriate accommodation must be based on the particular facts of each case. In selecting the particular type of reasonable accommodation to provide, the principal test is that of effectiveness, i.e., whether the accommodation will provide an opportunity for a person with a disability to achieve the same level of performance and to enjoy benefits equal to those of an average, similarly situated person without a disability. However, the accommodation does not have to ensure equal results or provide exactly the same benefits.

Q. When is an employer required to make a reasonable accommodation?

A. An employer is only required to accommodate a "known" disability of a qualified applicant or employee. The requirement generally will be triggered by a request from an individual with a disability, who frequently will be able to suggest an appropriate accommodation. Accommodations must be made on an individual basis, because the nature and extent of a disabling condition and the requirements of a job will vary in each case.

If the individual does not request an accommodation, the employer is not obligated to provide one except where an individual's known disability impairs his/her ability to know of, or effectively communicate a need for, an accommodation that is obvious to the employer. If a person with a disability requests, but cannot suggest, an appropriate accommodation, the employer and the individual should work together to identify one. There are also many public and private resources that can provide assistance without cost.

Q. What are the limitations on the obligation to make a reasonable accommodation?

A. The individual with a disability requiring the accommodation must be otherwise qualified, and the disability must be known to the employer. In addition, an employer is not required to make an accommodation if it would impose an "undue hardship" on the operation of the employer's business. "Undue hardship" is defined as an "action requiring significant difficulty or expense" when considered in light of a number of factors. These factors include the nature and cost of the accommodation in relation to the size, resources, nature, and structure of the employer's operation.

Undue hardship is determined on a case-by-case basis. Where the facility making the accommodation is part of a larger entity, the structure and overall resources of the larger organization would be considered, as well as the financial and administrative relationship of the facility to the larger organization. In general, a larger employer with greater resources would be expected to make accommodations requiring greater effort or expense than would be required of a smaller employer with fewer resources.

If a particular accommodation would be an undue hardship, the employer must try to identify another accommodation that will not pose such a hardship. Also, if the cost of an accommodation would impose an undue hardship on the employer, the individual with a disability should be given the option of paying that portion of the cost which would constitute an undue hardship or providing the accommodation.

Q. Must an employer modify existing facilities to make them accessible?

A. The employer's obligation under Title I is to provide access for an individual applicant to participate in the job application process, and for an individual employee with a disability to perform the essential functions of his/her job, including access to a building, to the work site, to needed equipment, and to all facilities used by employees.

For example, if an employee lounge is located in a place inaccessible to an employee using a wheelchair, the lounge might be modified or relocated, or comparable facilities might be provided in a location that would enable the individual to take a break with co-workers. The employer must provide such access unless it would cause an undue hardship.

Under Title I, an employer is not required to make its existing facilities accessible until a particular applicant or employee with a particular disability needs an accommodation, and then the modifications should meet that individual's work needs. However, employers should consider initiating changes that will provide general accessibility, particularly for job applicants, since it is likely that people with disabilities will be applying for jobs. The employer does not have to make changes to provide access in places or facilities that will not be used by that individual for employment-related activities or benefits.

Here is what JAN says about the job accommodation process:

The Job Accommodation Process[5]

With the existence of the Americans with Disabilities Act (ADA) and the Rehabilitation Act in the United States, an increasing need has developed to be knowledgeable about reasonable accommodations for people who have disabilities. Knowledge about reasonable accommodations can assist employers in hiring and retaining individuals who have disabilities. Some employers have the misconception that people who have disabilities are difficult to accommodate.

However, this is not necessarily true. Accommodations are typically low cost and easy to implement. Data collected by the Job Accommodation Network (JAN) provides evidence that employers who have instituted accommodations for people with disabilities have benefited financially. Reports show that more than half of all accommodations cost less than $500 and that most employers report benefits in excess of $5,000.

When considering accommodations for someone who has a disability, it is important to remember this process must be conducted on a case-by-case basis with input from the person who has the disability.

The person's abilities and limitations should be considered and problematic tasks must be identified. The following process used by the Human Factors Consultants at JAN can be a helpful tool in determining successful job accommodations. The need to research accommodations may arise in any stage of employment. Different stages may include the application, employment and return to work stages. An overview of the process with an explanation and examples of each step is provided.

The Job Accommodation Process as Used by JAN

Flowchart
Step 1: Define the problem.
Step 2: Is it possible to modify the job?
Yes—Revise the job description.
Step 3: Is it possible to modify the existing facility?
Yes—Modify the facility.
Step 4: Does a product or service exist that would solve the problem?
Yes—Purchase the product or service.
Step 5: Is it possible to use or combine available products differently than they are usually used?
Yes—Use and integrate the product.
Step 6: Is it possible to modify a product?
Yes—Modify the product.
Step 7: Is it possible to design a new product?
Yes—Design the new product.
Step 8: Are there alternative placement possibilities?
Yes—Reassign to available position.
Step 9: Redefine the situation.
Step 10: Maintain accommodations.

An Explanation of the Job Accommodation Process

Step 1: Define the problem.

Defining the problem correctly is the first step of the job accommodation process and is critical for successful results. Answering the following questions may be helpful when defining the problem.

What are the individuals' specific symptoms and limitations that are creating barriers to performing job tasks? Be specific. Remember that even individuals who have the same disability may have different limitations.

Is the person's condition progressive or stable? If progressing quickly, this may change the accommodation approach to some extent.

What degree do limitations affect the individual's job performance? Note that just because an individual has a disability or limitations does not necessarily mean that accommodations are needed. People who have disabilities may need no accommodations, a few or many. This must be considered on a case-by-case basis.

What specific job tasks are problematic and what specific equipment if any is typically used?

Does medical documentation need to be obtained? Medical information can be helpful in determining if the individual is a qualified person with a disability who has the right to a reasonable accommodation. It is also helpful when determining appropriate accommodations.

Step 2: Is it possible to modify the job?

Yes—Revise the job description.

Job modifications can include a shift change, schedule change, a flexible work schedule, the option to work at home or even sharing or trading job duties with another employee. Job restructuring of marginal duties may also be included. Listed below are examples of accommodation situations and solutions.

Situation: A data entry clerk had agoraphobia and had difficulty traveling during peak hours of traffic.

Solution: The employee's working hours were changed from 8:30 A.M.–4:30 P.M. to 10:00 A.M.–6:00 P.M. Cost of accommodation: $0.

Situation: A highly skilled electronics technician who has AIDS was taking large amounts of annual and sick leave.

Solution: The employer provided a flexible work schedule and redistributed portions of the workload. The company also instituted AIDS awareness training for employees. Cost of accommodation: $0.

Situation: As a result of diabetes, a productive employee in a retail business was experiencing fatigue and needed time during the day to administer medication. She was having difficulty performing her sales duties for a sustained period of time.

Solution: The employee's schedule was altered to allow for a longer meal break and periods during the day to administer medication.

Step 3: Is it possible to modify the existing facility?

Yes—Modify the facility.

Modifying the existing facility may include installing a fire alarm strobe with a flashing light for someone with no hearing or installing a ramp for someone with a mobility impairment to access an area where only steps are provided. Other modifications could include providing an accessible parking space to someone who easily fatigues or replacing doorknobs with door levers for individuals with limited grasping ability. Following is an example accommodation situation and solution:

Situation: A computer programmer in a manufacturing company is a person with cerebral palsy that affects her fine motor control. The employee uses a wheelchair and as a result could not access certain areas of the worksite.

Solution: A bathroom stall was enlarged and safety rails installed. The desk was raised several inches to enable the wheelchair to fit underneath, and computer space was made available on the first floor of the building. A ramp and automatic doors were installed and a personal parking place close to the elevator was identified. Building owners provided materials and absorbed costs for building remodeling. Cost to owner of the building was approximately $5,000.

Cost to employer: $0.

Step 4: Does a product or service exist that would solve the problem?

Yes—Purchase the product or service.

There are many different products on the market that can be used to accommodate individuals who have disabilities. Some products may be specifically designed and intended to accommodate individuals who have disabilities while others were not designed specifically for that purpose, but work nonetheless.

It is also important to remember that if a product is purchased as an accommodation that additional accommodations may be needed to support the individual in the use of that product. Additional accommodations may include proper training, maintenance of the device, and coworker support just to name a few. If the product is to be used with other equipment, compatibility with that equipment must be considered.

The purchase of a service may also be a form of accommodation. This may include an interpreter for an individual with a hearing impairment, a reader for someone with no vision or even the services of a company that can transfer information from printed text into alternative format. Listed below are example accommodation situations and solutions involving the use of products and services.

Situation: A file clerk with no hearing needs to have effective communication in a training seminar held for all new employees.

Solution: The employer hired a sign language interpreter for the employee's training which lasted two days. Cost of accommodation: $500.

Situation: An electro-mechanical assembly worker acquired a cumulative wrist/hand trauma disorder that affected handling and fingering. This decreased his ability to perform the twisting motion needed to use a screwdriver.

Solution: A rechargeable electric screwdriver was purchased to reduce repetitive wrist twisting. Electric screwdrivers were subsequently purchased for all employees as a preventative measure. Cost of accommodation: $65.

Situation: A college professor with AIDS was having problems associated with the disability. His greatest difficulty was in grading students' papers.

Solution: A closed circuit television system was purchased which allowed him to magnify the print on the papers.

Step 5: Is it possible to use or combine available products differently than they are usually used?

Yes—Use and integrate the product.

This step of the process requires the accommodation seeker to consider products for uses in which they were not necessarily intended. For example, amplified stethoscopes were designed to assist nurses and doctors in noisy areas like an emergency room or on the site of an accident. However, these same amplified stethoscopes have also proven helpful to nurses and doctors with hearing loss in controlled noise environments. The following is an example of an accommodation situation and the solution.

Situation: An elementary school teacher with hearing loss was having great difficulty hearing students due to background noise of screeching tables and chairs on the tiled classroom floor.

Solution: The school system could not purchase carpeting for the classroom immediately, so the teacher was permitted to cut holes in tennis balls and place them on the legs of the tables and chairs. Although the tennis balls were not intended for this purpose, they eliminated the background noise of the screeching tables and chairs. Fortunately, the teacher had tennis playing friends who were willing to donate their used tennis balls. As a result, the cost of the accommodation was $0.

Step 6: Is it possible to modify a product?

Yes—Modify the product.

Employers can often modify existing products in-house, however, at times it may be necessary to call a professional such as a rehabilitation engineer, electrician, computer specialist or the manufacturer of the product. Following are examples of modification situations and solutions.

Situation: A catalog salesperson with a spinal cord injury had difficulties using the catalog due to finger dexterity limitations.

Solution: The employer purchased a motorized catalog rack. When modified with a single switch control, the employee was capable of turning the rack to access the catalog using a mouth stick. An angled computer keyboard stand for better accessibility was also provided. Cost of accommodation: $1,500.

Situation: A custodian with low vision was having difficulty seeing the carpeted area he was vacuuming.

Solution: A fluorescent lighting system was mounted on his industrial vacuum cleaner. Cost of accommodation: $240.

Step 7: Is it possible to design a new product?

Yes—Design the new product.

Step 7 involves designing a new product to satisfy the accommodation need. This may require the assistance of a professional such as a rehabilitation engineer, computer specialist, or a company willing to design a new product. The following examples of new products that have been designed were taken from the *Rehabilitation Engineering Tech Brief* published by The Cerebral Palsy Research Foundation of Kansas Inc.

Situation: A bicycle repairman was having difficulty bending down to work on bicycles as a result of a back injury.

Solution: The technicians at the Mobile Shop of the Cerebral Palsy Research Foundation designed and made an adjustable height bicycle rack that could raise and lower the bicycle to a comfortable working height. Seventy staff hours were required for design, fabrication and installation. Material and part costs for the modification totaled approximately $450.

Situation: A library clerk with a physical disability walked with crutches and as a result of her disability had limitations in shelving books that involved climbing and reaching. Balance was a problem when performing this task.

Solution: A book service cart with fold-up steps and handrails with a place for her to stow her crutches was designed and fabricated. Cost not identified.

Step 8: Are there alternative placement possibilities?

Yes—Reassign to available position.

Reassignment may need to be considered as a reasonable accommodation. If so, the Americans with Disabilities Act Technical Assistance Manual for Title 1 offers the following guidelines when considering reassignment.

Reassignment in general:

- Is only required of employees;
- May not be used to limit, segregate or discriminate;

- Does not require the employer to reassign an unqualified person;
- Does not require an employer to create a new job or bump another employee; and
- Does not require an employer to promote an employee with a disability as an accommodation.

Reassignment to a lateral (with similar pay/benefits) position only when:

- Accommodations are not possible for the current position; or
- Accommodations for the current position cause an undue hardship; or
- The employer and employee agree that reassignment is the more appropriate accommodation in the present job.

Reassignment to vertical (with less pay/benefits) position only when:

- There are no lateral vacant positions or
- There are no lateral vacant positions or soon to be vacant positions in which the employee is qualified to perform with or without reasonable accommodations.

Step 9: Redefine the situation.

If at the end of the accommodation process, an accommodation has not been identified, then an accommodation option may have been overlooked. At this point, it is suggested that the situation is redefined and an accommodation team assembled. An accommodation team may consist of medical specialists such as doctors, physical therapists, occupational therapists, nurses or pharmacists. The team may also include rehabilitation counselors/engineers and/or an organization that serves people with disabilities.

Step 10: Maintain accommodations.

Once an accommodation has been identified and provided, it is important to maintain it. When maintaining accommodations, it may be helpful to answer the following questions.

Are accommodations being evaluated for effectiveness?

Does the employee have good communication with the supervisor to report any problems that may arise with provided accommodation?

Has any change occurred with the employee's condition, limitations, work environment or job duties that would affect existing accommodations?

If a product was purchased as an accommodation then:

Is the product being used appropriately?

Was proper training provided to the person using the product? Is proper maintenance to the product being performed? Are other accommodations needed to support the use of the product?

Is support being offered to the person with the disability to sustain the accommodations that were implemented?

What Does JAN Mean for You?

The Job Accommodation Network offers help to anyone involved in the process of ensuring that accommodations are made so that an individual can perform either in the job they are currently employed to do, or are being hired to do. As the information provided in this chapter indicates, JAN offers assistance on guidelines and provides definitions for important concepts like "reasonable accommodation" and "undue hardship." Some of the major problems that individuals with limitations experience are not caused by the actual physical barrier, but stem from attitudes toward and/or misunderstandings about making accommodations.

By being aware of possible accommodations or the process of determining those accommodations, you can make the difference in the likelihood of keeping your job or perhaps being hired for a new one. But remember that you cannot force someone to change the way they think or handle their business, unless they have discriminated against you in some way. If you do your homework and research the company and a particular job for which you are applying, it may help you when it comes down to the hiring decision. And just as important, if you are presently employed, you will have a better idea of the accommodation process and the ways that it may be possible to ensure you can continue to do your present job.

Some of the situations offered in this chapter may not apply to someone who has a chronic illness rather than a disability; however, sometimes an accommodation works in a number of situations. Therefore, I have included the material as it was written on the JAN

Web site. JAN does have some detailed accommodations for specific conditions on its Web site (www.jan.wvu.edu/links). According to the January 1–March 31, 2000, quarterly report, the three Web sites specific to a condition that received the largest number of "hits" (or visitors) were for accommodations for fibromyalgia, psychiatric disability, and fragrance sensitivities. The JAN report suggested that those seeking information on accommodations for these conditions preferred the anonymity of the Internet rather than approaching their employers.

Notes

1. Job Accommodation Network, "History & Mission of JAN: Impact." www.jan.wvu.edu/english/history.htm. Last updated March 13, 2000.

2. Job Accommodation Network, "What Is JAN?" www.jan.wvu.edu/english/whatis/htm. Last updated Jan. 19, 2001.

3. Job Accommodation Network, "Congressional Report, July 26, 2000." www.jan.wvu.edu/media/2000Congress.html.

4. U.S. Department of Justice Civil Rights Division, U.S. Equal Employment Opportunity Commission, "Americans with Disabilities Act, Questions and Answers," July 1996.

5. Job Accommodation Network, "Job Accommodation Process." www.jan.wvu.edu/media/JobAccommodationProcess.html.

CHAPTER Seven

Working for Yourself: Is Self-Employment for You?

Like many other situations that individuals with disabilities face, there is both good news and bad news for those interested in self-employment or starting a small business.

Self-employment offers many benefits for people with disabilities:

- The freedom, flexibility, and independence that come from working for oneself.

- The opportunity to work in a disability-friendly environment.

- The ability to reduce the need for transportation.

- The ability to accommodate changing functional levels.

- The ability to create an accessible work environment.

- Individuals with disabilities who receive income support, such as Social Security Disability Insurance (SSDI) or Supplemental Security Income (SSI) disability payments, can increase their income while still staying within the income and asset requirements of those programs.

However, anyone considering entrepreneurship must also be aware of the challenges involved in starting a business, which range from attitudinal barriers to lack of coordination among federal programs:

- The possible loss of cash benefits from SSDI or SSI disability programs, and perhaps even from a private disability program

- The possible loss of health-care benefits such as Medicare or Medicaid

- The inability to get credit because of poor credit ratings

- The lack of assets to use as collateral

- The lack of access to programs promoting self-employment and small business development

- Government disability programs that overlook entrepreneurship as an avenue from the public rolls to self-sufficiency

The 1999 passage of the Ticket to Work and Work Incentives Improvement Act addresses some, but not all, of these issues. If you are receiving some form of disability benefit, be sure to check for the latest regulations on income levels and retention of health benefits. President George W. Bush's announcement of the Freedom Initiative urged that many different agencies of the government work together in increasing the resources and services available to those with disabilities. That includes the right to assistance, not only for employment, but also self-employment. I cover the Social Security Administration's Ticket to Work program in the next chapter as part of a discussion of education and training, because the majority of individuals will need some form of vocational rehabilitation before they are able to return to work. One important note to remember is that the program started in 2002 in just a few states, and it will take some time to work out all of the problems that are bound to occur in a new program of this magnitude.

The Importance of Small Business in America

With more than one million new businesses each year, America's economy depends on small businesses for its vitality and growth. According to the 1997 report of the U.S. Census Bureau, the nation's 17 million small, nonfarm businesses constituted 99.7 percent of all employers, employed 52 percent of the private workforce, and accounted for 51 percent of the nation's sales. Industries dominated by small business provided 11.1 million new jobs between 1994 and 1998, virtually all of the new jobs created during that time period. Small businesses are most likely to generate jobs for young workers, older workers, and women, provide 67 percent of first jobs, and produce 55 percent of innovations.

Although the U.S. Small Business Administration (SBA) establishes industry-specific definitions, it generally considers any business with fewer than 500 employees, including self-employed individuals, to be a small business. The Federal Reserve Board's report, *National Survey of Small Business Finances (1995)*, found that small businesses were home based 53 percent of the time. Twenty-four percent of all new businesses in 1993 began with no outside financing. The remaining 76 percent received funding from traditional sources, such as banks, credit unions, and finance companies, or from family members or credit card advances.

Although some reports have stated that 80 percent of all small businesses fail within five years, statistics from the U.S. Census Bureau reveal a different story. The Census Bureau reports that 76 percent of all small businesses operating in 1992 were still in business in 1996. In fact, only 17 percent of all small businesses that closed in 1997 were reported as bankruptcies or other failures. The other terminations occurred when the business was sold or incorporated, or because the owner retired.

I'd Rather Be Working for Myself

Because of the problems that individuals often encounter in finding employment, they may turn to self-employment, either in a desperate attempt to survive financially or as an outgrowth of an activity they have enjoyed doing. As I mentioned previously, some of my work efforts came from things I was already interested in, such as leather artwork. I liked burning images onto leather and then framing it and soon had requests to sell some of the results.

Thousands of people with disabilities have been successful as small business owners. The 1990 national census revealed that people with disabilities have a higher rate of self-employment and small business experience (12.2 percent) than people without disabilities (7.8 percent). The type of business that a person with a disability can operate is limited only by imagination. The University of Montana Research and Training Center on Rural Issues for People with Disabilities has documented that entrepreneurs with disabilities have successfully operated a wide variety of businesses, such as the following: accounting service, air-conditioner repair service, auction service, auto body repair shop, bakery, bicycle shop, boat-making shop, child-care service, chiropractic practice, contract service, counseling service, farming, freelance writing, janitorial/maintenance service, piano-refinishing service, real estate office, restaurant, used clothing store, weed abatement service, and welding shop.

There are essentially three sources of information on starting your own business: the government, at all levels; published information found in books, magazines, and online; and your own research. The federal government, in particular, has gone to a great deal of effort to make this information available to you, and it is usually free. If you do decide to become self-employed, you will appreciate that last fact, as you'll have other things on which you will need to spend money.

In my research, both for this book and other projects, I have found that almost all information from the government on small business, self-employment, and individuals with disabilities is available both in print and online. If you have access to the Internet, you can research, download, and print out whatever information you need. If you do not have a computer and Internet access, check with your local library. Most libraries now provide their patrons with Internet access, and they may also have print copies of the various publications put out by the SBA and the Department of Labor. If the publications are not available in the library, you should be able to order them either from the Government Printing Office or from the specific agency. (Many are free, but others may have a charge.)

The list of books, magazines, and Web sites provided in Appendix A covers everything from the initial research steps in determining whether you should go into business for yourself to helpful suggestions to ensure your business runs smoothly. I have had some of these sources in my library for years and others I have found in doing my research for this book.

Research is the first step that anyone contemplating either self-employment or opening a small business should take. Once you have completed the self-evaluations in Chapters 1 and 2, you should have a better idea of what you want to do and what you can do, physically and mentally. Now it is time for the "legwork" to begin. If you have an idea of something that you want to do as a business, you must research that idea. I'll go into more detail of how to do that later in this chapter.

What Does the Government Offer?

Unfortunately, most of the various government employment programs, especially those of the federal government, haven't been directed toward self-employment. The Social Security Administration's new Ticket to Work is supposed to offer the individual the option of finding work he wishes to do, including self-employment. In the past, vocational rehabilitation offices tended to be overworked and the goal they strived toward was placing their clients in an employment position. The reasons are varied and tied into the bureaucracy itself. Vocational rehabilitation is covered in more detail in the next chapter, but I feel it is also important to bring it up here. According to the Rehabilitations Services Administration (RSA) statistics for 1997, only 2.7 percent of the 223,668 vocational rehabilitation clients with successful closures became self-employed or started a small business. However, RSA's own recent demonstration programs on client choice reported that 20–30 percent of their participants chose self-employment.

Small Business Self-Employment Service

When it comes to providing information specific to those with disabilities, the best place to start is with the Department of Labor, Office of Disability Employment Policy's Small Business Self-Employment Services (SBSES). The SBSES provides comprehensive information, counseling, and referrals about self-employment and small business ownership opportunities for people with disabilities. Entrepreneurship provides the opportunity for people with disabilities to realize their full potential while becoming financially self-supporting.

About SBSES[1]

SBSES answers questions from people with disabilities, service providers, friends and family of people with disabilities as well as anyone else with an interest in promoting self-employment and small business as career choices for people with disabilities.

The knowledgeable staff of the SBSES can provide information and referrals about:

Starting a Business

- Developing a business concept
- Market research
- Writing a business plan

- Obtaining capital
- Loan guarantees

Managing a Business

- Technical assistance resources
- Growing a business
- Personnel management
- Financial management
- Developing a marketing plan

Disability Issues

- Social Security
- PASS plans
- Health care
- Working at home

The information which is available from SBSES, as with all services provided by the Office of Disability Employment Policy, is free of charge and all communications are confidential. SBSES is staffed by the Job Accommodation Network (JAN).

The SBSES World Wide Web site, http://www.janweb.icdi.wvu.edu/ sbses, includes links to other entrepreneurship sites, including the Small Business Administration and state vocational rehabilitation programs. It also provides information on a variety of other technical assistance resources for writing business plans, financing, and other issues specific to developing a small business. Contact can be made by phone, mail or e-mail, or through the Web site. Small Business and Self-Employment Service, Job Accommodation Network, P.O. Box 6080, Morgantown, WV 26506-6080, Phone: 800-526-7234 V/TT, Fax: 304-293-5407 URL: http://www.jan.wvu.edu/ SBSES. Email: kcording@wvu.edu.

All information is free and all communications are confidential. The telephones are answered Monday through Thursday from 8:00 A.M. to 8:00 P.M. and Friday from 8:00 A.M. through 7:00 P.M. (Eastern Time). Voice mail records messages after hours, weekends, and holidays.

The SBSES Web site includes an extensive list of links to other resources, such as other government programs, nonprofit organizations, consumer protection resources, state vocational rehabilitation offices, as well as disability and small business Web sites and publications.

The Office of Disability Employment Policy has initiated a range of activities with other federal agencies to ensure that federal employment programs for people with disabilities will promote small business ownership as a career option, and that potential entrepreneurs with disabilities know about the process and resources for starting a business. Information on these programs can be obtained from the Office of Disability Employment Policy's Web site, www.dol.gov/dol/odep.

Small Business Administration

The SBA provides a tremendous amount of information for anyone wishing to start a small business as well as assistance once the business is up and running. However, it comes up short in offering information that is specific to those with disabilities.

For example, by clicking on a link on the SBA's Women's Business Center, you are directed to a "Disabled" Web page with reference to one book, which is out of print, and with links to the World Institute on Disabilities, the Montana University Rural Institute on Disability, Social Security Administration Bold Business Consultants, and the SBA home page. In the general information section, there are four paragraphs that cover some statistics on people with disabilities who are entrepreneurs and the advantages of self-employment. Then there are six questions on disabled entrepreneurs, which give very little information that is not found in more detail on SBSES.

However, once you get past what is missing at the SBA, you can immerse yourself in what *is* there, and the amount of information offered is amazing. Here are some of the topics covered online:

■ *Starting.* This section provides complete, step-by-step instructions to begin a business, including a start-up kit; business plan; training; counseling; online classes in such areas as business plans and raising capital; and BusinessLINC, a service that puts new entrepreneurs in touch with available business mentors. The section also contains free e-mail business counseling offered by SCORE (Service Corps of Retired Executives) at www.score.org.

■ *Financing.* This section gives detailed information on loan and equity-investment programs. It includes SBA loan forms that you can fill out online or download, free SBA online financial workshops, and free downloadable financial shareware for use in your business.

■ *Expanding.* This section offers growth opportunities, such as PRO-Net for online government solicitations and procurement opportunities; ACE-Net for growing businesses seeking angel investors; SUB-Net at www.sba.gov/subnet for subcontracting opportunities with large companies; and Trade Mission OnLine, a database of small businesses that seek to export their products, at www.sba.gov/tmonline/.

■ *Offices and Services.* This section describes programs devoted to women; veterans; minorities; networking; disaster assistance; the national Welfare to Work Initiative; and HUBZones, a program designed to provide federal contracting opportunities for qualified small businesses located in distressed communities.

■ *Local SBA Resources.* This is a listing of local SBA offices; contacts; and the services they provide to local businesses, including a local calendar of events for workshops, seminars, and other programs.

■ *Your Government.* This section contains Internet links to Web pages of the White House; Congress; the U.S. Business Advisor; as well as federal and state agencies, including the U.S. Patent Office, the U.S. Census Bureau, the Internal Revenue Service, and individual state home pages.

■ *Online Library.* This section provides specialized areas for the laws and regulations pertaining to small businesses, SBA publications, reports, statistics and studies, and communications with Congress.

■ *Outside Resources.* This section has Internet links to all sorts of business resources, ranging from financing and business schools to search engines, trade shows, and business travel.

SBA offices are located in all fifty states, the District of Columbia, Puerto Rico, the U.S. Virgin Islands, and Guam. For the office nearest you, call 1 800-U ASK SBA; fax: 202-205-7064; e-mail: answerdesk@sba.gov; TDD: 704-344-6640. You can also ask for the location of the following resources: Business Information Centers, Tribal Business Information Centers, One-Stop Capital Shops, Services Corps of Retired Executives, Small Business Development Centers, U.S. Export Assistance Centers, and Women's Business Centers. The Web site address is www.sba.gov.

The SBA publishes the following questionnaire, to help you determine whether starting a business is the right decision for you:

Ask Yourself: Is Entrepreneurship for You?[2]

There is no way to eliminate all the risks associated with starting a small business. However, you can improve your chances of success with good planning and preparation. A good starting place is to evaluate your strengths and weaknesses as the owner and manager of a small business. Carefully consider each of the following questions.

Are you a self-starter?

It will be up to you—not someone else telling you—to develop projects, organize your time and follow through on details.

How well do you get along with different personalities?

Business owners need to develop working relationships with a variety of people including customers, vendors, staff, bankers and professionals such as lawyers, accountants or consultants. Can you deal with a demanding client, an unreliable vendor or cranky staff person in the best interest of your business?

How good are you at making decisions?

Small business owners are required to make decisions constantly, often quickly, under pressure, and independently.

Do you have the physical and emotional stamina to run a business?

Business ownership can be challenging, fun, and exciting. But it's also a lot of work. Can you face 12-hour work days six or seven days a week?

How well do you plan and organize?

Research indicates that many business failures could have been avoided through better planning. Good organization—of financials, inventory, schedules, production—can help avoid many pitfalls.

Is your drive strong enough to maintain your motivation?

Running a business can wear you down. Some business owners feel burned out by having to carry all the responsibility on their shoulders. Strong motivation can make the business succeed and will help you survive slowdowns as well as periods of burnout.

How will the business affect your family?

The first few years of business start-up can be hard on family life. The strain of an unsupportive spouse may be hard to balance against the demands of starting a business. There also may be financial difficulties until the business becomes profitable, which could take months or years. You may have to adjust to a lower standard of living or put family assets at risk.

It's true, there are a lot of reasons not to start your own business. But for the right person, the advantages of business ownership far outweigh the risks.

Published Sources: Books and Magazines

An entire industry has grown up around the concept of starting your own business. Books, magazines, newsletters, Web sites, workshops, seminars, and conferences all deal with self-employment and/or starting a small business. There are also a large number of scams that promise easy money with little effort. Unfortunately, the only easy money is usually what you pay to them for information that is incorrect, incomplete, or impossible to carry out. So how do you find your way around all of this information, gathering accurate information about possible business opportunities without going broke? Here are a few tips.

Always check for references from legitimate sources, such as the Small Business Administration, the Small Business Development Centers, and local colleges and universities.

Spend time at your local bookstore, looking through the titles on small business and self-employment. Check for positive reviews on the back cover or inside. Those reviews should come from sources that you recognize or can check out easily. Consider a book like *The Work at Home Sourcebook*, 7th ed., by Lynie Arden. Any book that has gone into seven editions obviously has been well done and kept up to date. On the back cover there are quotes from three reviews: "Excellent" from *Parents Magazine*; "A comprehensive classic" by *Home Office Computing*; and "Useful for ideas about at-home jobs as well as job leads" from *Good Housekeeping*. This book is one to look through to determine whether the information it contains applies to your situation, and if you can afford it, buy it.

Look for authors with strong credentials. Sarah and Paul Edwards have written ten books on working at home with over a million copies in print. I have nine of the ten, having purchased the first one in the mid-1990s. Their writing is clear and well focused, and they include plenty of examples. One of their most recent is a title in the "Books for Dummies" series, *Home-Based Business for Dummies*. Both the "Books for Dummies" and the "Idiot's Guide To" books can usually be considered good sources for information in clear, down-to-earth writing, regardless of the specific topic.

Some books target a specific niche within the work-at-home market, such as *Mompreneurs Online: Using the Internet to Build Work@ Home Success* is by Patricia Cobe and Ellen H. Parlapiano. According to the back cover, the two women are considered authorities on working from home and have appeared on *Oprah*, *NBC Nightly News*, CNN, CNBC, *Good Morning America*, Fox News Network, *Good Day New York*, Lifetime's *New Attitudes,* and National Public Radio, as well as others.

Sometimes you can judge a book by its publisher. *The Home Office and Small Business Answer Book*, 2nd ed., by Janet Attard, is published by Henry Holt and Company, which has been publishing books since 1866. It's possible that sometimes a book published by a reputable firm might not be helpful, but in this case, there are also several strong statements of praise for the first edition.

There are books on starting businesses for under $1,000; books on online businesses, mail-order businesses, and working by yourself; books that cover specific occupations, such as writing; and almanacs that simply provide information on hundreds of businesses with specific details on start-up costs and potential earnings.

Most large bookstores will have a complete section devoted to magazines on various types of businesses arranged by category. A word of warning here; some of the "opportunity" magazines may have some good articles but they may also have advertisements for questionable, get-rich-quick schemes. Remember the old adage, "If it sounds too good to be true, it probably is."

Online Sources

The same guidelines about using common sense and caution when evaluating printed material apply to Web sites. The primary problem with Web sites is that you might not be able to tell whether the information is legitimate. One way of verifying the source is to check with trade associations and nonprofit organizations. Generally, if you have followed a link from one of the government's sites, the Web site you reach should be fine. Another resource to check is the small business Web sites at About.com, Yahoo.com, and AOL.com.

Personal Research

This last section is devoted to research that you need to do personally. Hopefully, you have come up with some idea of what you want to do. If that is the case, then it is time for you to look around you and find out whether there is a need for your business idea. You can have the best idea in the world, but if no one is interested in buying your product or service, it won't do you any good. If you have taken advantage of the SBA's local office or the Small Business Development Center's services as well as met with a representative of SCORE, you should have a good understanding of market research.

There is another way to find ideas for a business. Listen to people around you. Be observant. Sometimes the need for a product or service is very evident, but no one has taken the time to follow up on it. I recently read an article about a young Marine onboard one of the U.S. Navy warships stationed in the Indian Ocean. The ship had been in port in Australia when the war with Afghanistan began. Instead of returning to the United States on schedule, the ship is now serving as a launching pad for helicopters with no return date set. The Marine had just completed extra computer training and is now turning that into a profit. He is burning music CDs as well as doing computer servicing for his shipmates. His wife buys him blank CDs at a bulk rate and ships them to him. He saw a chance to provide a service and make some money. What can you do with an entire neighborhood, town, or city or more to check out for business opportunities?

There are some ideas that sound good and that initial research seems to indicate could be moneymakers. Make sure that you do enough checking. They may require a large amount of capital investment, they may take more to develop and get off the ground than you have the physical energy and ability to do, or they may just be one of those ideas that sound good but whose time just hasn't come yet.

A Market to Consider

Do you have a need for some product or service that hasn't been met? My first book, *When Muscle Pain Won't Go Away*, arose from my questions about fibromyalgia (FM). During the five weeks that I spent in the hospital, after I found my rheumatologist and he was able to give me a definite diagnosis, I had a lot of questions about FM. But almost nothing had been written about fibromyalgia for the patient or the doctor in 1987. Finally, Dr. Rubin told me, "You're a writer, write a book."

It was easier said than done, but I did begin research at the medical library. By the time I found a publisher in 1990, there had only been about 200 articles published in medical journals. I sat down and wrote out all of the questions that I had been asking Dr. Rubin and others that I wanted answers to that would not only inform me about FM but also help me to live with it. I sold the book based on a proposal, which is an outline of the book and a statement about the demonstrated need for it. The book is now in its third edition in a trade paperback edition and Barnes & Noble brought out a hardcover reprint last year.

This book is an example of seeing a need and working to meet it. I've already talked about how I've managed to earn a living through the years. I'll probably come up with hundreds of other ideas that I won't have the energy or the desire to follow up on. While I was writing this book, I thought of a good many more possible projects.

What I would like to suggest to you is that you consider a potential $1 trillion market that is still being ignored by many in today's businesses. According to the National Organization on Disability, people with disabilities are often overlooked when it comes to marketing goods and services. And I don't necessarily mean such items as wheelchairs. My own experiences over the last fifteen years have shown me areas that need to be addressed. Some are included in the Americans with Disabilities Act; others are really common-sense matters that haven't occurred to someone unless he or she has experienced them personally.

For example, I need a way to manage shopping by myself, particularly if I'm just buying a few items. When I used my electric scooter, I had plenty of room. I carried my purse in the front basket and had room for a soft drink can as well. I had the area around my feet, where I could put small items. Actually, I could get quite a few items on the scooter if I worked it right. But now with my electric wheelchair, I need one hand for the controls and one hand for my purse or the door. I tried buying a little fold-up bag with two wheels, but it was always twisting around or getting caught in the door. Of course, I didn't have a free hand to open a door when I was pulling the bag. I've switched to a rolling backpack as a purse. I now have room to place paperback books or other small items inside, besides what I usually carry in a purse. Still I need to set the backpack on my lap or on my footrest when I go in or out of doors, though I do get lucky a lot and meet someone coming out or going in who holds them open for me.

Something that frustrates me is being able to get to merchandise, and I haven't found a solution yet. I tell the store personnel that if I can't see or check out merchandise, I can't buy it and it is a lost sale on their part. I have found friendly salesclerks who will often go out of their way to help me, but sometimes I just prefer to look by myself.

Buying groceries and then getting them into the house is a real problem. I've had offers of help from many other shoppers as well as store staff, but I'm not comfortable with the idea of having someone follow behind me while I try to decide if I want to buy the fried chicken in the deli or the cheaper brand of bread. I do have others help put my purchases into the van, but getting them out of the van and into the house is becoming more and more difficult. Something even more frustrating is getting the trash down the wheelchair ramp and to the curb. A friend has tried adapting several things in the house already but without luck. I do have wheels on my large trashcan, but pushing it down the ramp while in my wheelchair is rather challenging. That trashcan doesn't steer worth a darn and neither does the little four-wheel wire basket that I use to transport the groceries. If anyone has any good ideas, I'll be glad to include them in the next edition of the book.

Have you found a better way to do something because of your chronic illness? Remember, although there are an estimated 54 million Americans with disabilities, there are nearly 90 million who have chronic illnesses. That makes an even wider market. Of course, you have to find something that is needed by a definite niche. Whether their chronic illness has led to a disability or not, people still have varied interests and characteristics. If you found something that would be needed or desired by even one-half of one percent of chronically ill people, you would probably make a fair amount of money. Think about it.

Notes

1. The Small Business and Self-Employment Service, "About SBSES." www. jan.wvu.edu/SBSES/about.htm.

2. U.S. Small Business Administration, "Small Business Start-up Kit." www.sba. gov/starting/ask.html. Last modified Jan. 6, 2002.

PART III

Education, Training, and Going to Work

CHAPTER Eight

Education and Training

W hen we begin to face the changes that chronic illness (CI) makes in our lives, we often find that the skills or abilities we have been using to make a living are no longer available to us. It doesn't matter if we have several advanced degrees or not even a high school diploma; suddenly, everything we've known how to do has become something that we can no longer count on.

Most CIs do not appear overnight. Their symptoms may creep up on us, and it may take months or years for the symptoms to become serious enough to affect our work. That doesn't mean there are not some illnesses that strike severely without a lot of warning, only that the majority show up and gradually worsen until we realize that we must do something about our work and our lives. We need to do three things: rethink, refocus, and retrain.

Rethink

Change is very hard for most of us to accept. Even when our lives are already undergoing change, we tend to drag our feet and resist it with all of our might. This applies to everyone, not just someone facing a chronic illness or disability. Individuals who undergo serious spinal cord injuries may continue to insist they will walk again, despite medical evidence to the contrary. We tend to hold on to broken marriages and unhappy work situations essentially because we don't want to exchange what is familiar for what is unknown.

The time comes, however, when we know that we must move on; either we will take charge and make the change or it will be forced upon us. For those with CIs, it may be that our bodies simply call a halt to our continued efforts to remain at a level of activity beyond what our body can manage, or the push may come from an outside source. Our employer may step in and sever the work relationship, calling it a layoff, downsizing, or just plain firing. The results, however, are the same.

It is then that we are forced to rethink our lives, from our expectations to our activities. Although there are some indications that Americans are stepping away from the concept, there are still a great many people who identify themselves by their job or career. When we lose that job or career, by whatever means, we lose a great deal of our identity. Beyond the job, those of us with CIs have also lost the ability to place physical or mental demands upon our bodies and have those demands met.

I worked to put myself through college, including joining the navy to participate in the G.I. Bill, which provided tuition assistance. Although I had help from the Veterans Administration and the Texas Veterans program, I always worked while going to school. If necessary, I worked more than one job. Later, when I had my public relations firm, I put in however many hours it took to get the work done, including a number of all-night sessions. But, I no longer have the physical stamina to put in an eight-hour workday, much less more. My body has betrayed me.

I truly believe this is the hardest part of coping with a chronic illness: the time when we finally know that we can no longer work two jobs, ride horseback, do the Texas two-step all night, or become the youngest CEO of a company. Realizing that you have to make new goals and accept much less than you had counted on can be very depressing, no matter what it was that you expected to do in life.

In Chapter 1, I asked you to determine your emotional state and mentioned the stages of grief. I have talked to a number of individuals with health problems who did not realize they had both the right and the need to grieve for their lost health as well as the possible loss of their dreams. You must do this if you are to move forward. Grief is a natural process when we are faced with loss of any kind, not just death. Allow yourself the time to do this and then begin to rethink your future.

Rethinking can be difficult or it can be an exciting challenge. Think about how you felt when you were fresh out of high school or college, on the brink of beginning your career. You probably experienced a combination of excitement and dread. I felt this way when I joined the navy. I knew things would be difficult and very different from what I was accustomed to. I was the first woman in my small hometown to join the service, so I had no one to give me a real idea of what I would be doing.

Boot camp turned out to be less difficult for me than I had expected. I soon realized that self-discipline was at the core of doing well. I learned what was expected of me and then did it, including jumping off the "elephant." This was a high diving board, equivalent to the height one would jump from the deck of a navy ship. It didn't matter that at that time women weren't allowed on ships; we still had to jump off, inflate our dungarees, and stay afloat for a certain period of time in order to graduate from boot camp. Doing this was a major achievement because I was afraid of heights, and, though I could swim, I really didn't have the endurance to swim very far. I remember thinking as I stood on that diving board that this was just an order that I had to obey, and once I completed the exercise, I probably wouldn't ever have to repeat it. So I did it.

No one is telling you to jump off the side of a navy ship. But you may feel that what you now face is just as bad or worse, because it isn't a onetime, short-term deal. You must now rethink your life, perhaps only a small part of it, perhaps a very large part of it, depending upon the extent of your CI and its impact upon your life and ability to work.

With the evaluation and research you did in previous chapters, now you are ready to take some definite steps in finding that new work. You are rethinking your life's plan.

Refocus

If there are parts of your education and training from your past work that you can use in your future work, that is good. It will save you time, energy, and money. If you must completely change directions, you will probably require some new education and/or training. In this chapter you look at the types of education and training that are available and what will suit your particular need.

Now you must decide what you want, which you established with the goal-setting exercises in Chapter 3, and focus on what it will take to reach that goal. As you do your research on what it will take to get started in your new adventure, you will begin to refocus your way of thinking. You will learn to take into consideration the restrictions that your health has now placed on your activities. Even new education and training must be evaluated within the context of your health.

A very important question must be answered as you consider new education or training: Can you afford *not* to get it? Time and again as I did my research for this book, I found that one of the problems that many employers faced with new employees, disabled or not, was the lack of qualifications and training. The workplace is changing and workers must change with it or face being forced out completely. Remember the stipulation in the Americans with Disabilities Act: "The individual must be qualified to perform the *essential functions* of the job, with or without reasonable accommodations."

You must have the qualifications, including any necessary training, for whatever job you are considering. If you hope to go to work for someone else, that person will look at your education and training as well as your previous experience and expect you to have the level of competence such a background indicates. If you are going to be self-employed or open your own small business, you must know what you are doing or you will fail before you even get started. So how do you obtain the knowledge and skills that you will need in your future work?

Retrain

Gaining new knowledge and skills can be very informal or very formal and structured; it can be expensive or not so expensive. You must first decide what you need to prepare yourself for your new occupation.

One example of a situation in which the knowledge and skills can be learned in a more informal manner is in some of the arts and crafts. Some people tend to dismiss this field as a way of making a living because they equate handmade with poor quality. However, the opposite is more likely, especially if the artisan has taken the time to really learn their art and take pride in their product.

Earlier in the book, I mentioned a friend of mine who makes ceramic items to sell for the Christmas market. She has invested quite a bit of time and money in both her equipment and the development of her pieces, insisting that only the best ones will be offered for sale. She began working with ceramics as a hobby, something that she enjoyed doing just for herself. Soon, however, she found that she was getting requests from friends and coworkers for items. She didn't attend any classes to learn how to make her ceramics; she taught herself the process and watched others as they worked on theirs. Then she spent time learning by trial and error until now she seldom has to reject a piece because it doesn't meet her standards, and she can paint one Christmas ornament in about an hour. She prices each ornament at $5 and generally sells all that she makes for the holiday season.

On the opposite end of the spectrum is someone who must obtain a degree in order to work in a new profession. An example would be someone who has decided to work as a psychotherapist to patients with CI. She already has her own experience to help her, but if her degree is in education or history, it won't help her meet the requirements for getting a license to practice.

Once you have decided that you need training, either on your own or as part of a medical treatment or a vocational rehabilitation program, how do you get it and, most important, how do you pay for it? We address these issues in the next sections.

Books, Magazines, and Published Sources

I admit that I am an avid reader. My house has so many books that they ought to provide insulation all on their own. Whenever I take on a new project or even consider beginning one, I start with books. My first stop is usually the library to see what is available that can help me determine if I want to move forward with the project or drop it. Writers of both fiction and nonfiction are always being asked where we get our ideas. For us it's not so much a matter of getting ideas as it is identifying those that will work out and those that should be dropped immediately.

I feel the same way about my projects for making money. I start out with quite a few ideas and begin looking into them. I may decide that it will take more money than I have on hand right now to get started in the new project, and it may take some time to earn back the cost of education and start-up. If that is the case, and my interest in the project isn't strong enough, I will stop right there before I have done more than basic elementary research.

If I decide to pursue the project a bit further, I will look for magazines published on the topic. When I worked on Western-style key chains and jewelry, I picked up a few instruction sheets as well as books at the local craft store. Many of these contained instructions, patterns, and color pictures. I also paid a visit to the local used bookstore, Recycled Books and Tapes, on the square in Denton, which carries books from all types of nonfiction to everything in fiction except romance. I found quite a few books on gems and jewelry making as well as some on marketing crafts.

The next stop is the local Barnes & Noble or Borders, where I can look over the books to determine which ones will help me. Although it is nice to buy some books online, especially if I know the author, I prefer to buy my reference books where I can look them over. I spend so much on books that I want to make sure that I will be able to use the information inside.

Workshops, Seminars, Conferences, and Community Education Classes

Most communities offer some sort of community education classes through the local school district, the city parks and recreation department, and, if there is one, a community education department at the local college or university. If you don't have a high-school diploma, check out the GED (General Educational Development) tutoring and testing that is often offered through these community sources or perhaps even through the public library.

If you have not graduated from a high school or you don't have a notarized transcript for home school, you must have a GED certificate before you can apply and be accepted by most colleges and universities. Even then some will require you to take a test to prove that you are capable of learning at the college level. In Texas, it is the Texas Academic Skills Program (TASP) test, but there are a number of exemptions you may meet. Check with the particular institution you wish to attend.

Here are some examples of courses in various subject areas offered by the Denton Independent School District for fall 2001:

■ *Computer Skills and Information.* Typing & Keyboarding; Introduction to Word Processing; Windows 95 (Intro) for Senior Adults; Microsoft Office 2000; Microsoft Excel (in beginning, intermediate, and advanced levels); Microsoft PowerPoint (beginning, intermediate, and advanced); Designing a Web Page; How to Buy a Computer; Introduction to "Surfing" the Internet; and "Surfing" the Internet (intermediate).

■ *Business and Investments.* Planning to Retire? Financial Steps for Today; The Power of Personal Financial Control; Investments for Women; Financial Well-Being! What Every Woman Should Know; and Market Outlook 2001: Turning Information into Opportunity.

■ *Creative Arts and Sewing.* Silk and Floral Designs; Beginning/Intermediate Quilting: Machine & Hand Tying; and The Art of Watercolor I. (I know that the instructor of the watercolor class has fibromyalgia, but she still manages to paint and have her own studio and gallery.)

■ *Leadership and Career Development.* Interviewing Techniques; Business Writing; "This Job's for You" (taught by a licensed professional counselor and sponsored by the North Central Texas Workforce Center, operated by North Texas Human Resource Group); Real Estate: Principles and Practices I and II; Law of Agency; Law of Contracts; Understanding Real Estate Math; and Modern Marketing.

In Denton, we also have classes taught by the City of Denton Parks and Recreation Department, North Central Texas College (a community college), and the University of North Texas School of Community Service. North Central Texas College offers classes and associate degrees as well as certificates in some of its technical and vocational programs. Classes include everything from farm and ranch management to computer sciences to occupational therapy assisting, nursing (including both registered nursing and licensed vocational tracks), welding, and law enforcement.

Depending on where you live, you may be able to attend conferences and/or workshops that specialize in what interests you. Check with the local newspaper, the chamber of commerce, the school district, or the nearest college or university for more information. You might also check at the library to see if there is an association or organization that focuses on jewelry making, dog training, or whatever you are interested in pursuing. Sometimes these groups will hold conferences that also include training opportunities. Quite often, small business organizations will offer workshops in various topics.

Colleges, Universities, and Distance Learning

The next level of education or training is to seek a degree or certification from a college or university. Until the advent of the Internet and e-mail, the only way to attend a college or university was to move to the town or city where the institution was located and spend three, four, or more hours a day sitting in one classroom after another for sixteen weeks at a time. That doesn't even count the "lab" classes that provided students with more "hands-on" learning.

But now many institutions of higher education are facing a decrease in the "traditional student," the one who entered college right after graduating from high school and who then spent four years obtaining a bachelor's degree in whatever field he or she chose. Those traditional students have been decreasing in number partially because of demographic changes. After the baby boomer generation aged, there was a decrease in the number of children. However, many schools had built up their campuses to meet the needs of those born from 1946 to 1964, only to find they now don't have enough students to utilize the space. So the forward-thinking schools began to look beyond the "traditional" student for a new "student market."

They found one market in older individuals who chose to attend college for the first time or to return to college now that their children were older or grown. Those older students often felt somewhat awkward among the younger people but soon found they had something to offer—their experiences in the workforce.

When I returned to college after leaving the navy and realizing that I was unable to have children, I was only in my twenties, but I had served three years in the navy and I had worked since my discharge. When I heard about Governors State University, it had been open only three years. The university promoted itself as a nontraditional university. The most obvious difference was that students could get credit for life experience toward what is called the Board of Governors Degree. This was what I wrote about when discussing the self-evaluation in Chapter 2. I received credit for all of the training the navy gave me as well as the actual work that I did while I was in the navy.

Today there are many other colleges and universities that allow credit for life experience. After all, someone in upper management who has worked her way up through the levels to her present position already has a great deal of knowledge that goes beyond what a textbook can offer. It is foolish to demand that this person take a basic business management course as part of getting a degree, when she could probably have written the textbook for the class.

When you have completed your self-evaluation in detail, you may want to see if you can apply any of it toward a college degree, if that is your new goal. It may be possible for you to attend that college or university as a regular student. But what if moving to the school's location will put a major dent in your finances or is simply not possible because of other demands? Then what?

You may want to consider "distance learning." In the past the term would have been applied to correspondence courses, and until recently only a few accredited colleges offered such courses. Now the Internet has given educational opportunities to a lot of people who would not have been able to take advantage of learning because of the physical distance or other commitments.

On its Web site, www.usdla.org/04_research_info.htm, the United States Distance Learning Association in Needham, Massachusetts, defines distance learning as ". . . the acquisition of knowledge and skills through mediated information and instruction. Distance learning encompasses all technologies and supports the pursuit of life-long learning for all. Distance learning is used in all areas of education including Pre-K through grade 12, higher education, home school education, continuing education, corporate training, military and government training, and telemedicine."

The Distance Education Clearinghouse at the University of Wisconsin-Extension offers this definition among others on its Web page (www.uwex.edu/disted/definition.html): "Distance Education is instructional delivery that does not constrain the student to be physically present in the same location as the instructor. Historically, Distance Education meant correspondence study. Today, audio, video, and computer technologies are more common delivery modes. The Distance Learning Resource Network (DLRN) provides this definition by Virginia Steiner."

If you want to consider distance learning but don't necessarily want to attend one of the larger, well-known universities, you might want to check with either of the groups mentioned above or read a book such as the *Bears' Guide to Earning Degrees by Distance Learning,* written by John B. Bear, Ph.D., and his wife, Mariah P. Bear, M.A. (see the resources section of Appendix A). The book provides information on those legitimate educational institutions that offer distance learning as well as information on determining the legitimacy of a business or school that offers degrees, diplomas, or other study.

Vocational Rehabilitation

Essentially there are two ways to get the training or education that you will need for your new career: someone else pays for it, or you do. Even if you have to pay for it yourself, there are places to go for financial help. Let's look at the possibility of someone else paying for it or providing it first.

Generally if you require help in obtaining a new job or career because health problems have forced you to stop working, you may be eligible for vocational rehabilitation. The U.S. Department of Labor says the objective of vocational rehabilitation is to empower individuals with disabilities and to prepare them for work. Vocational rehabilitation services are provided by both public and private agencies. Individuals who become disabled as a result of military service or during military service are most often provided rehabilitation services through the U.S. Department of Veterans Affairs.

The Ticket to Work and Work Incentive Improvement Act was passed in 1999 and made major changes in how both individuals with disabilities and those without disabilities can find work. Before this act, every state had programs operating, but a person might have to go to several different departments or agencies all at different locations to file for unemployment benefits if he lost his job, to register for finding employment through the state agency, to apply for vocational rehabilitation, or to get help in managing a career. To help solve those problems, the act created America's One-Stop Career Center System.

America's One-Stop Career Center System

America's One-Stop Career Center System connects employment, education, and training services into a coherent network of resources at the local, state, and national level. This new system links the nation's employers to a variety of qualified applicants and provides job seekers with access to employment and training opportunities next door and across the country.

You can check with the local office, whatever its title, for more information on scholarships and training. For those individuals who are eligible, training services may include occupational skills training, on-the-job training, training programs operated by the private sector, skill upgrading and retraining, entrepreneurial training, job readiness training, adult education and literacy activities, and customized training. For individuals with disabilities, vocational rehabilitation is a required partner for the one-stop system, so those with disabilities can access the full range of services provided by the vocational rehabilitation agency.

Assessing an individual's aptitudes, abilities, and attitudes is the first step in vocational rehabilitation. The process includes medical, psychological, and vocational testing. The assessment provides the information needed to set up a rehabilitation plan, which might include physical, occupational, speech, or hearing therapy. Job-seeking skills, such as interviewing and resume preparation, are included. Finally, after an individual is placed, most vocational rehabilitation services follow up to ensure that the job match is successful. Although the process that the government agencies use may not be as extensive as what I suggest in this book, they are set up to help those who qualify for vocational rehabilitation.

While there may be a few differences in qualification criteria from one state to another, essentially the criteria are about the same. I will give the information from the Texas Rehabilitation Commission (TRC) as an example. The program helps Texans who have physical or mental disabilities prepare for, find, or keep employment. A person is eligible if his disability results in substantial problems in getting employment; vocational rehabilitation services are required by that person to prepare for, get, and/or keep a job; and that person is able to get and/or keep a job after receiving services.

The Vocational Rehabilitation Program serves people with a wide variety of disabilities, some of which are mental illness, hearing impairment, impaired functioning of arms or legs, back injury, alcoholism or drug addiction, mental retardation, learning disability, and traumatic brain injury. Depending upon the individual client's level of disability, she may be eligible for one or more of the following services:

- Medical, psychological, and vocational evaluation

- Counseling and guidance to help in planning vocational goals

- Applicable medical treatment, including hospitalization, surgery, and therapy to lessen or remove the disability

- Assistive devices such as artificial limbs, braces, wheelchairs, and hearing aids to stabilize or improve functions on the job or at home

- Rehabilitation technology devices and services to improve job functioning

- Training to learn job skills in trade school, in college, at university, on the job, or at home

- Training to learn appropriate work behavior if necessary

- Job placement assistance to find jobs compatible with the person's physical and mental ability

- Follow-up after placement to ensure job success

The vocational rehabilitation agencies in each state are also responsible for adjudicating claims from those within their states who are applying for Social Security disability payments. Sometimes, there are so many claims to be handled that the number of individuals who are referred by their doctors or who seek help from the agency might have to wait for some time before they are able to see the caseworker.

After I moved to Denton and realized that I couldn't work even part-time, I applied to TRC for help. Because there was nothing that could be done surgically or medically beyond what my doctors were already providing, we skipped that part of the evaluation. The caseworker and I discussed fibromyalgia, and what I wanted to do, which was write. He was able to get a chair for me to use at the computer and at the desk that was adjustable in all sorts of ways. Later when I ended up having to spend quite a bit more time in bed, TRC provided me with a notebook computer so I could write in bed. That was all that I had requested and felt that I needed, because I knew I wanted to write. I also wrote up a business plan as a guide for my efforts.

The purpose and intention of the federal and state agencies that are responsible for vocational rehabilitation sound very good and they have helped many individuals. However, my experience aside, much of what I hear from others about the state vocational rehabilitation agencies and even the Veterans Administration vocational rehabilitation tends to be negative. The primary complaint seems to be related to the usual problems with a large bureaucracy. The reports reflect long waiting periods, little choice in selecting a future occupation, a definite reluctance to agree to self-employment, and little or no follow-up. Like many other government agencies, there are not enough workers to handle the number of claims.

With that said, I want to encourage you to use the government agencies if you are entitled to the assistance. Pursue the matter not as if your life depends on it, but your future does. That means to be "assertive," but not "aggressive." You must do your part as well. Remember that you are an active partner, not only in managing your health care but also in the shaping of your future. If you don't know which options you want to pursue, do some research. Then, discuss them with your caseworker. Never blame that person for failure if you have not held up your end of the commitment.

Social Security Disability and the Ticket to Work

Individuals receiving Social Security disability benefits are being offered new vocational rehabilitation opportunities as a result of the Ticket to Work program. When I first heard about the changes the Social Security Administration (SSA) was making in the disability program and that it was introducing the Ticket to Work (TTW), I was very impressed and hopeful. I am still hopeful. The program seems to be the answer to what I consider a major drawback for the SSA disability program.

The Social Security Administration has admitted in some of its literature that individuals cannot live on the disability check that it provides. The amount of each disability check is based on how much a person has made while working, but the average monthly check is around $500. I don't know of any part of the country where a person can buy housing, clothing, and food with that amount, let alone cover other expenses such as transportation and medical care.

Before the new TTW program was actually begun, a series of hearings were held around the country to allow both rehabilitation specialists and individuals to address their concerns about the program. There were many, ranging from the age that a person qualifies for the TTW to who would be eligible to be considered for the Employment Network, and from the periodic reevaluation of a disability that is a part of the Social Security disability program to the continuation of Medicare Part A for those people with disabilities who also work.

Medicare coverage is an important issue. With all of the problems that exist with Medicare, such as a two-year waiting period for it to kick in after a person goes on disability, no coverage for prescription drugs, and the increasing number of doctors who do not accept Medicare, it is still certainly better than no health-care coverage at all. There isn't room in this book to debate the issue of health-care insurance for every American, but people with chronic illnesses have a demonstrated need for medical care, and thus the risk of losing their Medicare coverage is a major reason that people who qualify for disability payments often do not attempt to find employment.

The Social Security Administration established a twelve-member volunteer panel to provide suggestions on the TTW program, and this panel looked over the hundreds of concerns that were voiced at the public hearings and then made suggestions to address the concerns. It is vital that the SSA remain open to the concerns about the TTW as it starts being implemented and throughout the coming years. One positive note that I see with the program is that it is voluntary. No one who is drawing disability is forced to take part.

The TTW program is different from the recent Welfare-to-Work program, which has enabled many individuals to move from welfare to work while still drawing some assistance from the government. In that case, most of those on welfare were *required* to go to work. However, problems began to arise in late 2001, because some of those in the program who were nearing the end of their entitlement to assistance were also among the thousands of individuals who had been laid off during the economic downturn.

It is difficult enough for those with disabilities to find work during a recession without facing the danger of losing both their disability payments and health benefits. If a person with a disability has neither a job nor government benefits, knowing there may be a turnaround in six months doesn't feed, house, or clothe that person nor does it provide needed medicine. Let's hope that the Ticket to Work program does work and helps individuals get back to work with dignity and to work they choose to do.

To give you more background on the provisions of the Ticket to Work program, the following is from the "Ticket to Work Program Questions and Answers" page of the Social Security Administration's Web site:

I. The Ticket to Work Program[1]

What is the Ticket to Work Program?

The Ticket Program is something new in SSA. The program will offer SSA disability beneficiaries greater choice in obtaining the services they need to help them go to work.

When will the Ticket Program begin?

Before we officially begin this major new program, SSA must develop final regulations. Most beneficiaries in the first thirteen states listed below will receive Tickets early in 2002, once the regulations are effective.

Will the Ticket Program start everywhere at the same time?

No. SSA will phase in the Ticket Program over a three-year period. During the first year of operation, which will begin in early 2002, the program will be available only in the following thirteen states: Arizona, Colorado, Delaware, Florida, Illinois, Iowa, Massachusetts, New York, Oklahoma, Oregon, South Carolina, Vermont and Wisconsin.

In the second phase, we will expand the program to these twenty additional states: Alaska, Arkansas, Connecticut, Georgia, Indiana, Kansas, Kentucky, Louisiana, Michigan, Mississippi, Missouri, Montana, Nevada, New Hampshire, New Jersey, New Mexico, North Dakota, South Dakota, Tennessee and Virginia, as well as in the District of Columbia. We intend to implement this phase later in 2002.

In the third phase, the program will be available in the remaining seventeen states: Alabama, California, Hawaii, Idaho, Maine, Maryland, Minnesota, Nebraska, North Carolina, Ohio, Pennsylvania, Rhode Island, Texas, Utah, Washington, West Virginia and Wyoming, as well as in American Samoa, Guam, the Northern Mariana Islands, Puerto Rico and the Virgin Islands. We intend to implement this phase in 2003.

The program will be operating in the entire country by January 1, 2004. So, people will receive their Tickets at different times.

How can I get more information about the Ticket Program?

SSA has contracted with MAXIMUS, Inc. to serve as the Program Manager for the Ticket Program. MAXIMUS will help us to manage the program. You can get information about the Ticket Program by calling MAXIMUS at their toll-free numbers, 1-866-968-7842 (1-866-YOURTICKET) or 1-866-833-2967 TTY (1-866-TDD 2 WORK).

How will I know where the Ticket Program is available?

We will announce our plans in many different places where people who receive Social Security disability benefits get information about

SSA, including Social Security's Internet web site, www.ssa.gov. You also can contact MAXIMUS at the numbers listed above or, if you can use the Internet, you can find this information at their web site, www.yourtickettowork.com.

What will a Ticket look like?

The Ticket will be a paper document that will have some personal information about the person receiving it and some general information about the Ticket Program.

How will I get my Ticket?

We will send the Ticket in the mail, along with a notice and a booklet explaining the Ticket Program.

If I get a Ticket, do I have to use it?

No. The Ticket Program is voluntary.

Where would I take my Ticket to get services?

You would take your Ticket to an Employment Network or to the State Vocational Rehabilitation Agency. The Employment Networks will be private organizations or public agencies that have agreed to work with Social Security to provide services under this program. As of mid-November, 2001, we have approved 185 organizations to operate as Employment Networks in the first thirteen States.

How will I find out about the Employment Networks?

You may contact MAXIMUS at the toll-free numbers shown above for information about Employment Networks that serve the area where you live. If you use the Internet, you can find this information on SSA's special "Worksite," www.ssa.gov/work and on MAXIMUS' web site, www.yourtickettowork.com. Also, some Employment Networks may contact you to offer their services.

How will I choose an Employment Network?

You can contact any Employment Network in your area to see if it is the right one for you. Both you and the Employment Network have to agree to work together. You are free to talk with as many Employment Networks as you choose without having to give one your Ticket. And you can stop working with one Employment Network and begin working with another one, or with the State Vocational Rehabilitation Agency.

If you need help in choosing an Employment Network, you may contact the Protection and Advocacy System in your state. You can call MAXIMUS at the toll-free numbers shown above for the telephone number and address.

II. Expanded Availability of Health Care Services

Does the new law include changes in health care coverage?

Yes. Starting October 1, 2000, the law extends Medicare Part A (Hospital) premium-free coverage for four and one-half years beyond the current limit for disability beneficiaries who work.

What about Medicaid?

The law includes several important changes to Medicaid. For example, it gives states the option of providing Medicaid coverage to more people ages sixteen to sixty-four with disabilities who work. To find out if this coverage is available in your state, call the state Medicaid office in your area.

III. Removal of Work Disincentives

Will you still review my medical condition?

SSA will not conduct a medical review of a person receiving disability benefits if that person is using a Ticket. Benefits can still be terminated if earnings are above the limits.

Starting January 1, 2002, Social Security disability beneficiaries who have received benefits for at least twenty-four months will not be medically reviewed solely because of work activity. However, regularly scheduled medical reviews can still be performed and, again, benefits terminated if earnings are above the limits.

If I go back to work, will I automatically lose my disability benefits?

No, the new law has not changed our work incentives rules.

For more information about Social Security's work incentives you should:

- call our toll-free number at 1-800-772-1213;

- contact your local Social Security office; or
- visit our special "Worksite" at www.ssa.gov/work

If my disability benefits stop because I go back to work, will I have to file a new application if I can't work anymore?

Starting January 1, 2001, if your benefits have ended because of work, you can request that we start your benefits again without having to file a new application. There are some important conditions:

- You have to be unable to work because of your medical condition.
- The medical condition must be the same as or related to the condition you had when we first decided that you should receive disability benefits.
- You have to file your request to start your benefits again within sixty months of the date you were last entitled to benefits.

Will I have to wait for you to make a new medical decision before I can receive benefits?

No. We will make a new medical decision, but while we are making the decision, you can receive up to six months of temporary benefits—as well as Medicare or Medicaid.

If you decide that you are unable to start my benefits again, will I have to pay back the temporary benefits?

No.

What if I Don't Qualify?

It is possible that you may not qualify for help through the government vocational rehabilitation programs and yet it is also impossible to continue working in your current field. What do you do then? Although it may be difficult to get training and education on your own, you aren't completely without the possibility of some assistance. The important point is that you recognize the need for retraining. The lack of skills and training has been a major problem in hiring people who have disabilities. It is actually a problem for many others whose jobs are being eliminated through changes in the workplace. Computer technology is making a difference in some areas but there are other causes for the changes that are taking place.

This is one of the reasons that I suggested that you check out the *Occupational Outlook Handbook* for those jobs and professions where there is anticipated growth. Put this information together with your own self-evaluation and then find out what kind of training you need. There is help available to pay for further training and schooling.

Other Sources for Rehabilitation Services

Many universities and colleges that offer courses in vocational rehabilitation provide services to individuals in their communities. If you don't qualify for the state or federal programs, look for a university that offers degrees in vocational rehabilitation and see if you qualify for help with them.

There are also quite a number of private companies that also provide such services. Cost and type of services will vary. Check out such companies thoroughly, asking for references and association with national rehabilitation organizations.

Sources of Financial Aid for Retraining

There are two government departments that can provide you with help in finding financial aid for retraining: the Department of Education and the Department of Labor. Start your online search at www.firstgov.gov and click on "Online Services for Citizens," which will take you to a new screen. On the left side of the screen will be a place for you to "Select a topic." Click on that, and choose "Education/Jobs." The page that opens will give you a number of choices, such as "Education," "Jobs," and more.

You can also check out America's Learning eXchange (ALX), Your Guide to Learning Resources, which can be reached through the Web page above or by going directly to www.alx.org. The Learning Xchange connects users to career development, training and education, and employment resources, all of which are important to remain competitive in today's workforce. ALX is one of four complementary, Web-based services offered to the public through America's Career Kit. ALX is supported by many professional training and educational organizations dedicated to providing the knowledge, expertise, and constituent networks to ensure that users find the resources they need.

Another source for financial aid can be found on the AskERIC

Web site. ERIC is an educational database. ERIC can be accessed directly at http://www.askeric.org. At the top of the screen, there are several options; click on "Topic A-Z," and then choose the letter "F." The page will then list several options; click on "Financial Aid." This will lead you to a long list of links and topics, and you may find several that will be relevant to your specific situation.

There will be a number of links for you to follow but probably the most helpful is "Creating Options: A Resource on Financial Aid for Students with Disabilities (2001)." This resource paper is published by HEATH Resource Center, the national clearinghouse on postsecondary education for individuals with disabilities. Previously located at the American Council on Education, HEATH is now located at George Washington University in Washington, D.C. The paper includes information on four types of aid: grants, or aid that generally does not have to be repaid; loans, which must be repaid (usually with interest) over a specified period of time (usually after the student has left school or graduated); work-study employment, which enables a student to earn money toward a portion of school costs during or between periods of enrollment; and scholarships, which are gifts and awards based on a student's academic achievement, background, or other criteria. I have included some of the resources in Appendix A, but I can't include the entire paper because of space. I urge you to go online and print out the paper. If you do not have online access, call HEATH at 1-800-544-3284 for information on how to get a copy. If you look further into the resources listed in this report, you will probably find some sources for financial help that will apply to you specifically.

Scholarship Scams

Please beware of the many scholarship scams that are being advertised both online and in print publications. Most of the time you can find the information yourself free. There are several different ways the scams operate, but in almost every case, you must pay something in advance. Sometimes you get information that is totally useless; other times you never hear from the service again. Often the scams will use official-sounding names containing words such as *national, federal, foundation,* or *administration.* For more information on such scholarship scams, go to http://www.ftc.gov/bcp/conline/edcams/scholarship/.

Note

1. Social Security Administration, "Ticket to Work Program Questions and Answers." www.ssa.gov/work/ResourcesToolkit/legisregQA.html.

CHAPTER Nine

Finding That Job

I've already mentioned being realistic when talking about goal setting. And although I want you to be realistic, that doesn't mean that you can't strive for something that you really want to do. What I mean by being realistic is that you must have the basic job skills necessary for a particular job *and* you must be able to perform the activities of the job with "reasonable accommodations."

I would love to have any of a number of jobs, but I know that with my physical limitations of low energy and chronic pain, I won't be able to hold them. I have always wanted to go into space, however, every time I see those astronauts experiencing the effects of gravity during their launch into space, I shudder. If they can ever find a way of getting us up there without dealing with the force of gravity, I'll be ready to go; until then, I'll stay here on earth.

There are other jobs that have certain physical requirements that must be maintained for the safety of the employee and those around them. We must be honest with ourselves and not seek or apply for a job that we know we cannot do, not even with accommodations.

Barriers to Employment

A number of studies have been done in recent years on the difficulties that individuals with disabilities face in finding employment. The Department of Labor's Office of Disability Employment Policy (ODEP) provides summaries of some of these studies on its Web site as part of its *Education Kit 2001* "Statistics About People with Disabilities and Employment."[1] I highlight two of them in this section.

The Urban Institute, in Washington, D.C., used information from the Disability Supplement of the National Interview Survey (NHIS-D) to look at barriers to employment for adults with disabilities.[2] It reported the results when 16,000 persons with disabilities

154

were asked about their disability, their work, and their need for accommodation. The researchers used the respondents' self-reports of specific activity limitations to define disability. By this definition, the researchers calculated that there were 11.3 million working-age adults (ages 18–64) with disabilities, of whom 37 percent were working in 1994–1995.

The researchers separated the sample into two categories: "high likelihood" to work, defined as those for whom accommodations will enable work or who reported their disabilities would not prevent them from working; and "low likelihood," defined as those who reported they were retired from work or could not work even with accommodations.

More than half of the nonworking adults with disabilities who were studied encountered difficulties. The most frequently cited reasons for being discouraged from looking for work were:

No appropriate jobs available 52%

Family responsibilities 34%

Lack of transportation 29%

No appropriate information about jobs 23%

Inadequate training 22%

Fear of losing health insurance or Medicaid 20%

Discouraged from working by family and friends 14%

Sometimes there are very legitimate reasons why we do not or cannot seek work, either full-time or part-time. But let that decision be yours; don't let someone else force that decision upon you.

Need for Work Accommodations

I covered the job accommodation process in Chapter 6, but I want to add a bit more information here. In the NHIS-D survey described above, both persons with disabilities who were working and those who were not working stated a need for similar types of accommodations. One-third of nonworking persons with disabilities reported the need for some type of accommodations. The other two-thirds could work without accommodations or *were unaware of specific accommodations that might make it possible to work.*

The most common accommodations cited were:

Accessible parking or accessible public transit stop nearby   19%

An elevator 17%

Adaptations to work station 15%

Special work arrangements (reduction in work hours,
reduced or part-time hours, job redesign) 12%

Handrails or ramp 10%

Job coach 6%

Specific office supplies 5%

Personal assistant 4%

Braille, enlarged print, special lighting, or audiotape 2%

Voice synthesizer, TDD, infrared system or other technical
device 2%

Reader, oral or sign language interpreter 2%

A second survey, conducted by Cornell University and also summarized in the DOL *Education Kit 2001*, indicates how employers are doing when it comes to hiring and making accommodations for workers with disabilities. It reports on two research initiatives that examined employer practices in response to the employment provisions of Title I of the Americans with Disabilities Act and related civil rights legislation. Cornell interviewed by phone a random sample of human resource and equal employment opportunity personnel from the public and private sectors.

Listed below are the eleven areas of accommodations and five access needs of applicants outlined in the study and the percentage of employers who stated they had made accommodations in these areas.[3]

The types of accommodations that employers made were:

	Private	*Public*
Made facilities accessible	82%	93%
Had flexible human resource policy	79%	93%

Restructured jobs/work hours	69%	87%
Made transportation accommodations	67%	86%
Provided written job instructions	64%	69%
Modified work environment	62%	93%
Modified equipment	59%	90%
Made reassignment to vacant position	46%	58%
Provided readers and interpreters	36%	79%
Changed supervisory methods	35%	55%
Modified training material	31%	49%

The types of access provided to people with disabilities included:

	Private	Public
Wheelchair access	82%	95%
Time flexibility in test taking	45%	39%
Communication access for hearing impaired	43%	91%
Communication access for visually impaired	37%	77%
Removing volatile/scented substances	32%	48%

Employer Attitudes

In the Cornell survey, respondents were also asked to rate seven possible barriers to employment and advancement of people with disabilities. Both the public and private sector employers saw lack of related experience as the biggest barrier.

The seven barriers listed are outlined below:[4]

	Private	Public
Lack of related experience	49%	53%
Lack of required skills/training	39%	45%

Supervisor knowledge of accommodation	31%	34%
Attitudes/stereotypes	22%	43%
Cost of accommodations	16%	19%
Cost of supervision	12%	10%
Cost of training	9%	11%

When asked how they, as employers, might reduce employment and advancement barriers, the top six answers were:

	Private	*Public*
Visible top management commitment	81%	90%
Staff training	32%	71%
Mentoring	59%	71%
On-site consultation/technical assistance	58%	71%
Short-term outside assistance	41%	43%
Employer tax incentives and special budgets	26%	69%

The employers also saw difficulty in making workplace changes in the following areas:

	Private	*Public*
Changing the attitudes of coworkers and supervisors	32%	33%
Modifying their return-to-work policy	17%	11%
Creating flexibility in the performance management system	17%	15%
Changing the leave policy	10%	8%
Adjusting medical policies	7%	9%
Ensuring equal pay and benefits	2%	4%

In summarizing these reports, the Department of Labor concluded that the key areas that need to be addressed are:

- Improvement in the education and training of persons with disabilities

- More outreach on the part of the employment community to recruit persons with disabilities

- A better understanding of reasonable accommodation

- A concerted effort to break through the attitudinal barrier that is so detrimental to full integration of people with disabilities into the employment arena[5]

Unlike physical and systematic barriers, attitudinal barriers among employers that often lead to illegal discrimination cannot be overcome simply through laws. The best remedy is familiarity, getting people with and without disabilities to mingle as coworkers, associates, and social acquaintances. In time, most of the attitudes will give way to comfort, respect, and friendship.

Strive to do your part in smoothing that integration. Try to be patient with those who don't understand and do all you can to keep the lines of communication open with your coworkers and your supervisors. Many people are afraid that they will "do or say the wrong thing" around someone with a disability. They therefore avert their own discomfort by avoiding the individual with a disability. As with meeting a person from a different culture, frequent encounters can raise the comfort level.

You can't change a potential employer's attitude if you aren't prepared to balance your side of the equation. You must do everything possible to present yourself as the qualified employee who is right for the job and you must be qualified and able to perform the job. You must do your homework about the job and understand its tasks and requirements as well as learn about any possible accommodations that would enable you to carry out the job.

How Do You Conduct a Successful Search?

Once you have completed the exercises in the earlier chapters dealing with your work experience, interests, and then your goals, it is time for you to begin actually looking for a specific job in the area of your interest.

When you begin looking for a job, you might check in the usual places such as the newspaper classifieds or trade publications. There is a better chance of finding a job in the trade publications than in the newspapers. I often read the classified ads in the newspaper just to get a feel for the overall picture of the city or the Dallas–Fort Worth metropolitan area. You can tell a lot about what is happening from what jobs are—and aren't—being advertised.

People do get hired through classified ads in the newspaper, but today there are a number of alternative ways to seek employment and you need to be prepared to use them all. The Department of Labor's Office of Disability Employment Policy publishes a number of helpful fact sheets on its Web site, including job searching, interview tips, and resume tips. The following three documents come from that site:

Essential Elements of an Effective Job Search[6]

What Job Seekers with Disabilities Need to Know

Whether you are entering the workforce for the first time, returning to the job market, or seeking advancement, the challenges of a job search are similar. Your goal is to find the position that best meets your needs. You must be qualified and able to sell yourself as the best applicant for the job(s) for which you apply. Here are some tips that can help you in meeting your job search goal.

Know Thyself

Have a strong sense of who you are. Know your assets and how to market them to employers.

Commit to Lifelong Change

Follow job trends. Take the initiative to maintain cutting edge skills that match changing employer requirements.

Be Computer Literate

Increasing your technical computer skills increases your marketability in the job market. Conduct online job searches. Visit employer Web pages and key job sites such as:

- CareerPath: http://www.careerpath.com/
- America's Job Bank: http://www.ajb.dni.us
- Monster Board: http://www.monster.com/
- CareerMosaic: http://www.careermosaic.com/

Update Your Resume Often

Customize your resume to reflect the assets you bring to each job. Use key words that can be electronically scanned by potential employers to positions you want. Reflect continuous employment in your skill area. Summer employment should support your field of interest. Volunteer or obtain temporary jobs if you are unemployed. Select a resume format that minimizes any gaps in employment.

Be Your Best

Locating a job is a full time endeavor. Give full attention to all that you do. Errors will knock you out of the running.

Be Organized

Have a written personal plan for vertical and lateral growth opportunities. Know what you must do each day to move closer to your goal. Stay focused.

Expand Your Network

Maintain and continuously strive to broaden your network. If you are working, network inside the company. Join professional groups.

Research Job Trends and Companies

Select targets of opportunity that match your skill areas. Request and study annual reports of select companies. Reflect each company's image in all communications with each company's representatives. Make good use of library resources. Read trade journals and business publications.

Have a Positive Attitude

A pleasant personality is a necessary asset. Your eagerness to adapt and to be a team player is essential. Show that you are flexible. A sense of humor and positive attitude are pluses.

Disclose a Disability Only as Needed

The only reason to disclose a disability is if you require an accommodation for an interview or to perform the essential functions of a particular job. Your resume and cover letter should focus on the abilities you bring to the job, not on your disability.

Be Prepared to Conduct an Effective Interview

Look your best from head to toe. Dress conservatively. Be brief and to the point when answering interview questions. Maintain a demeanor of success and reflect the company image when you respond. Have full confidence in what you bring to the employer and show how your skills meet the company's specific hiring needs. Ask thoughtful questions about the job and the company. NEVER say anything negative. Follow up immediately with a thank you letter or e-mail transmission.

Remember

Push yourself to go the extra mile in your job search and you will find the opportunity you are seeking.

This tip sheet was prepared in cooperation with the Business Leadership Network (BLN), a program of the Office of Disability Employment Policy. The BLN is a national program led by employers in concert with State Governors Committees that engages the leadership and participation of companies throughout the United States to hire qualified job applicants with disabilities. This program offers employers pertinent disability employment information; a network of companies sharing information on specific disability employment issues; the opportunity to provide training and work experience for job seekers with disabilities; and recognition for the best disability employment practices. For more information on this program, contact the Office of Disability Employment Policy (202)376-6200 (V), (202)376-6205 (TDD), infoODEP@dol.gov.

Writing and Formatting a Scannable Resume[7]

What Job Seekers with Disabilities Need to Know

Because we are living in an information age where technology drives most interactions, resumes sent via E-mail and traditional paper are likely to be scanned for key information by a machine, not a human being.

What It Means to Have Your Resume Scanned by a Machine

Because employers receive more resumes than they can process efficiently, they are switching to text-searching or artificial intelligence software to track resumes. These systems use optical scanners to put resumes into the computer which then searches for skills that match a job description. Optical character recognition (OCR) software looks at the image to distinguish every letter and number and creates a text file. Such systems are important because they significantly lessen the time it takes to search for qualified applicants to fill a job. These systems can also help employers by creating a centralized resume pool in companies that have a decentralized human resource function.

Why Scannable Resumes Are Important to Your Search

In order to efficiently review resumes, an increasing number of employers are letting computers take the first crack at selecting a first round of applicants for certain jobs. Because computers are programmed to search for certain words, every word in a resume is important in the selection process. Artificial intelligence software "reads" the text and extracts important information such as your name, address, work history, experience and skills. A clear resume allows the scanner to obtain a clean image in order to maximize "hits" (when one of your skills matches the computer search).

How to Prepare a Resume That Will Scan to Jobs You Are Seeking

Following are important tips on making your resume "scan-friendly."

- Use a standard typeface such as Courier, Helvetica, Futura, Optima, Universe or Times with a point size of 10–14.
- Use black ink on white 8½ × 11 inch paper. Do not use colored paper.
- Use only capital letters or boldface to emphasize important information. Do not use italics, underlining, boxes, graphics, or horizontal or vertical lines.
- Avoid a two-column format or resumes that look like newspapers or newsletters.
- Use only a laser-quality printer.
- Do not fold or staple pages.
- If faxing, use fine resolution and follow up with a mailed original.
- Avoid "formatting peculiarities." If you use E-mail, save your file as "text only" or "ASCII" to avoid the possibility that your word processor and your prospective employer's word processor are incompatible. E-mail a copy of your resume to yourself to make sure it looks the way you meant it to look.

- Use "key-words" phrases, terms, industry jargon, and titles to describe your abilities. Describe your experience with concrete words rather than vague terms. Be sure to use state-of-the-art terminology to describe yourself. If you have been out of the job market awhile, research new developments in your field and use up-to-date terms to present your skills. Savvy job seekers often mimic the words a company uses in its help-wanted ads. The more skills and facts you provide, the more opportunities you have for your skills to match available positions.

- Be concise and truthful.

- Use more than one page if necessary.

- If you have extra space, describe your interpersonal traits and attitude. Key words could include: time management, team player, dependable, leadership, and responsibility.

- Use a keyword summary of your skills at the top of your resume to get the attention of robotic and human inspectors. For example, if you are looking for an entry level position in architecture, your keyword summary might include: BS in Architecture, internship experience with large commercial project, knowledge of AutoCAD, PhotoShop, AccuRender, 3-D Studio. Place your name on its own line at the top of the page. Use the standard format for your address below your name. Then list each phone number on its own line.

- For job search purposes you may choose to have two versions of your resume:

    - One to send for the computer to read (scannable format and detailed descriptors).

    - One for people to read during an interview (a creative layout, enhanced typography, and summarized information.)

- Be sure to proofread your resume before sending it.

How Hiring Managers and Recruiters Use Electronic Applicant Tracking Systems

Typically, hiring personnel set up a search request and tell the computer whether certain qualifications are required or desired. Many resume-scanning systems then rank the candidates they select from the system. Some of the leading systems place a number or percentage next to a candidate's name indicating how many of the manager's requirements are reflected in the resume.

As we move into the 21st century, it is important to use technology to find a job. If you push yourself to go the extra mile in your job search, you will find the opportunity you are seeking.

This tip sheet was prepared with the help of EDS. EDS participates in the Office of Disability Employment Policy's Business Leadership Network (BLN), a business-led initiative that aims to stimulate best disability employment practices and enhance employment opportunities for job candidates who happen to have disabilities.

Interviewing Tips for the Job Applicant[8]

The old adage "Knowledge is Power" is useful to keep in mind as you prepare for the job interview. In this context, knowledge means a number of things: know your own capabilities and limitations, what the job you want entails, what you can contribute to the job, and how to present yourself in the most positive manner.

There are several types of employment interviews. Being familiar with them can help you better prepare for your interview.

- **Patterned Interview**: a structured format in which certain predetermined areas are explored using questions which have been written in advance and that are asked of all interviewees.

- **Non-Directive Interview**: a flexible format which is more conversational and does not rely on questions written in advance. The interviewer becomes more of an active listener.

- **Group Interview**: a panel format in which members alternately ask questions of the applicant.

Interviews can be stressful events. These tips for the interview may be helpful:

- **Be Enthusiastic**: Show your interest in the job you are seeking and in the business. Smile. Speak clearly.

- **Be Yourself**: Don't put on an act. Being yourself can help you relax during an interview and cut down on stress.

- **Be Prepared**: Review your resume/job application before the interview to have it fresh in your mind, because it will be fresh in the mind of the person who interviews you. Carry a completed generic application with you. This will enable you to provide information that may be required and to complete an application form if it was not done before the interview.

- **Know the Organization**: Your knowledge of the prospective employer will contribute to the positive image you want to create. Research the organization before the interview: talk to others who work there; ask for information about the organization and for a job description when the interview is set up; use the public library's reference books on public and private organizations.

- **Be Honest**: Tell the interviewer about your work skills, strengths and experience, including any volunteer work you have done. If you haven't had a particular kind of experience, say so, but also indicate your willingness to learn new skills. You don't have to embellish the truth. Simply present yourself as a positive person with skills to offer the employer.

- **Look Your Best**: You will never get a second chance to make a good first impression. Dress appropriately for the type of job for which you are applying. Looking your best will make you feel more confident and more relaxed. It will also show the interviewer that you are serious about the job and about yourself.

Good luck! Don't give up if you don't get a job immediately. Keep trying. Look upon each interview as a learning experience which can help you land the job you want.

Think Outside the Box

Actually, thinking outside the box can work in both employment and self-employment situations. Considering everything you have compiled in your notebook, think about the type of company that you think you would be happy working for, considering locale, working conditions, and workplace style. Post your resume online, check out the online job offerings, and go to the government Web sites dedicated to helping you get hired.

Consider working for a temporary agency. These companies no longer furnish only office staff and casual labor. They include managers, scientists, pharmacists, teachers, and computer specialists. Often they can find just the job for you that will give you some experience in your future field. Sometimes those temporary positions can turn into permanent ones, once you have your foot in the door and have shown you can handle the job.

There are also a number of employment agencies that specialize in placing individuals with disabilities. They work with the companies to open doorways that you can then walk, or roll through.

Don't forget the America's One-Stop Career Centers. They now have everything in one place to make it easier to get some training as well as find a new job. Many of them even offer child care while you are there, so you don't have to find a baby-sitter.

"Work at Home and Earn Thousands"— Don't Be Fooled!

There is a saying that goes, "If something sounds too good to be true, it probably is." People with limitations on their ability to work are often prime targets for a way to earn money by working at home. When our symptoms wax and wane from one day to the next, working at a regular job is often very difficult. If we had a way to pace ourselves, so that we could rest when we got tired, or work harder when we felt better, we believe that we could manage.

And you see the offers everywhere. At one time, they would be in the regular help wanted ads of your local newspapers. Now you are more likely to find them under the classification of "Business Opportunity" in newspapers, in the "shopper" type of weekly classified ad papers, or in the back sections of magazines. Small signs may be posted on street corners with phone numbers or Web addresses and these eager scam artists have definitely moved with the advance in technology; offers may show up in your e-mail, by the scores or more.

The pitches vary just a bit. They may tell you that you can make money stuffing envelopes, setting appointments, reading books for publishers, doing medical billing, or selling through e-mail marketing. There may be some honest opportunities out there, but according to the Federal Trade Commission (FTC), there may not be any business opportunity at all, or you may have to pay in money and then get others to come into the business after you, which makes it an illegal pyramid scheme rather than a multilevel marketing business.

The medical-billing scheme is usually an attempt to get you to buy a prepackaged business—known as billing centers—which will enable you to provide such services as billing, accounts receivable, electronic insurance claim processing, and practice management to doctors and dentists. These scams also promise to provide you with the clients. In fact, you will have to find clients for yourself, and you will never be able to recover your investment of $2,000 to $8,000.

In the stuffing envelopes scheme, you can only earn money by turning around and "selling" the idea to friends and relatives. Assembly or craftwork somehow is never "up to standard," so you can't even recoup your money for the supplies, much less the hours you have spent on the project.

Other schemes under the business opportunity classification are vending routes, pay phones (or even phone cards), and display rack operations. Advertisements for these even show up on television. The business ads that seem to offer a great opportunity to earn large sums of money for just a few hours a week often sound very legitimate. After all, there are vending machines almost everywhere, and it's easy to see that someone comes into grocery stores, convenience stores, and such to stock the racks with everything from greeting cards to cigars. People must be doing this, and surely they are making money.

The problem (and illegal aspect) of these "opportunities" is that they promise something they cannot or do not offer—profits. They take customers' money up front and then never deliver any goods or equipment, or else they provide vending routes that don't have any chance of making money.

The FTC has several publications providing potential buyers with advice on how to evaluate the legitimacy of such offers. One such publication is "Could 'Biz Opp' Offers Be out for Your Coffers," available online at www.ftc.gov/bpc/conline/pubs/invest/vending.htm.

Spotting the Scams

How do you spot these scams? The FTC tells consumers to take the following steps to make sure the opportunity that they are pursuing isn't going to cheat them out of their money:

■ *Get It in Writing.* Get all earnings claims in writing. Be sure the information includes the number and percentage of recent or current clients who have earned at least as much as the promoter claims. If the promoter hesitates or refuses to give the information in writing, find another business opportunity.

■ *Check References.* Interview references provided by the promoter of the business opportunity. The FTC requires business opportunity promoters to give potential purchasers the names, addresses, and phone numbers of at least ten prior purchasers who live the closest to the potential purchaser. Talk to each prior purchaser in person, preferably at the location of his or her business. This may help reduce your risk of being misled by "shills."

■ *Check Documents.* Study the business opportunity's franchise disclosure document. Under the FTC Franchise Rule, most business opportunity promoters are required to provide this document to potential purchasers. It provides information about the company, including whether it has faced any lawsuits from prior purchasers or lawsuits alleging fraud.

■ *Check Complaint History.* Contact the attorney general's office, state or county consumer protection agency, and the Better Business Bureau in the area in which the business opportunity promoter is based and where you live. Ask whether there's a history of unresolved complaints. Remember that a complaint record may indicate questionable business practices, but a lack of complaints doesn't necessarily mean the promoter and the business opportunity are without problems. Unscrupulous dealers often change names and locations to hide a history of complaints.

■ *Call Other Companies.* If the business opportunity involves selling products from well-known companies, call the legal department of the company whose merchandise is being promoted. Find out whether the business opportunity and its promoter are affiliated with the company. Ask whether the company has ever threatened trademark action against the business opportunity promoter.

■ *Get Professional Advice.* Consult an attorney, accountant, or other business adviser before you put any money down or sign any papers. Entering into a business opportunity can be costly, so it's best to have an expert check out the contract first. If the business opportunity promoter requires a deposit, ask your attorney to establish an escrow account where the deposit can be maintained by a third party until a deal is made.

■ *Take Your Time.* Take the time to complete each of these steps. Promoters of fraudulent business opportunities are likely to apply high-pressure sales tactics to get you to buy in. If it's a legitimate business opportunity, it'll still be around when you're ready to decide.

If you suspect that a business opportunity promotion is fraudulent, report it to:

- The state attorney general's office in the state where you live and in the state where the business opportunity promoter is based.

- Your county or state consumer protection agency. Check the blue pages of the phone book under county and state government.

- The Better Business Bureau in your area and the area where the promoter is based.

The FTC works for the consumer to prevent fraudulent, deceptive, and unfair business practices in the marketplace and to provide information to help consumers spot, stop, and avoid them. To file a complaint, or to get free information on any of 150 consumer topics, call toll-free 1-877-FTC-HELP (1-877-382-4357), or use the online complaint form (www.ftc.gov). The FTC enters Internet, telemarketing, identity theft, and other fraud-related complaints into Consumer Sentinel, a secure, online database available to hundreds of civil and criminal law enforcement agencies in the United States and abroad.

Fraud on the Internet: A New Avenue for an Old Con

While the Internet has added a new dimension to our lives and improved our access to information, work, and entertainment, it has also allowed con artists to find another way of trying to cheat others. Many of the online scams are similar to those we've seen before: work at home, business opportunities that really only take our money, and even fraudulent charitable schemes. There are other ways in which the scams take advantage of the Internet and the very real opportunities that are present on it.

Examples range from false auctions to travel and vacation scams and credit card fraud. Those that apply particularly to the readers of this book, however, include multiple-level marketing, e-commerce sites that promise you can make money but fail to deliver, and even investment schemes. As with any other work or business opportunity, research it thoroughly, check with the Better Business Bureau or the FTC's Consumer Sentinel site, which allows the consumer to report Internet fraud. There are several publications published by the FTC specifically directed to the Internet and fraud. Check them out at www.ftc.gov/bcp/menu-internet.htm.

The Federal Bureau of Investigation (FBI), jointly with the Department of Justice and National White Collar Crime Center (NW3C) has created the Internet Fraud Complaint Center (IFCC). The IFCC is located in Morgantown, West Virginia, with a dedicated Web site, www.ifccfbi.gov, which gives consumers nationwide the ability to file Internet fraud complaints online. The IFCC allows the NW3C and the FBI to strive to:

- Develop a national strategy to address fraud over the Internet.

- Collect, manage, and disseminate fraud complaint information to aid preventive and investigative efforts.

- Provide law enforcement and regulatory agencies with analytical data to identify and address new fraud trends and help stem the rise of Internet fraud.

- Provide a mechanism for reporting fraud on the Internet.

- Ensure that Internet fraud complaints are directed to the appropriate law enforcement and regulatory agencies.

Work Is Out There and You Will Find It!

This chapter covered how to find a job; how to recognize physical and attitudinal barriers to employment; and how to acquire the skills, experience, and job know-how you need to land a job. I've wrapped it up by covering scams, particularly ones that are most likely to be attractive to those of us who find it difficult to obtain traditional jobs.

Some readers may interpret this chapter to be somewhat negative in tone. That is not my intention. Just as each one of us must face the reality of our chronic illness and the limitations it has placed on us, so must we face the reality of the job market. I would emphasize the reality of that job market to any group I were addressing, including young people trying to find their first jobs, people changing career fields at any point in their working life (perhaps as a result of layoffs in hard economic times), and those over fifty who are facing difficulties in obtaining a job because of their age.

That said, I am confident that if you do your homework and

prepare yourself for your job hunt by brushing up on your job skills, whether by getting education or training or by considering ways that accommodations can enable you to perform the necessary activities involved in the job you are applying for, you will find the job or work that you want. It may mean working for someone else or working for yourself, but you will find it, if you hang in there and keep trying.

Notes

1. U.S. Department of Labor, Office of Disability Employment Policy, "Statistics About People with Disabilities and Employment," *Education Kit 2001.* www.dol/gov/dol/odep/public/media/reports/ek01/stats.hm.

2. Loprest, Pamela, and Elaine Maag, *Barriers and Supports for Work Among Adults with Disabilities: Results from the NHIS-D* (Washington, D.C.: Urban Institute, 2001).

3. Bruyere, Susanne M., *Disability Employment Policies and Practices in Private and Federal Sector Organizations* (Ithaca, N.Y.: Cornell University, Program on Employment and Disability, School of Industrial Labor and Relations, Extension Division, March 2000).

4. Ibid.

5. U.S. Department of Labor, Office of Disability Employment Policy, "Statistics About People with Disabilities and Employment," *Education Kit 2001.* www.dol/gov/dol/odep/public/media/reports/ek01/stats.hm.

6. U.S. Department of Labor, Office of Disability Employment Policy Publications, "Essential Elements of an Effective Job Search." www.dol.gov/dol/odep/public/media/reports/ek97/element.htm.

7. U.S. Department of Labor, Office of Disability Employment Policy Publications, "Writing and Formatting a Scannable Resume." www.dol.gov/dol/odep/public/media/reports/ek99/resume.htm.

8. U.S. Department of Labor, Office of Disability Employment Policy Publications, "Interviewing Tips for the Job Applicant." www.dol.gov/dol/odep/public/media/reports/fact/intervw.htm.

CHAPTER Ten

Closing Thoughts

So much information and assistance is available for people with limitations from their chronic illness that this book could have easily grown to several volumes, but I have tried to direct you to the essential information you'll need, and guide you to where you can find more. In addition to making use of that information, there are things that you can do. When I am talking to people, whether in person, on the telephone, or online, I will often hear, "There's nothing I can do. My health is too bad."

I know that there are individuals who can't do much. I haven't included all of my own health problems in this book, but it is sufficient to say that over the last ten years, it has been one thing or another, with several surgeries and procedures. Frankly, to quote the title of a book on chronic illness, I'm "sick and tired of being sick and tired." Every time I try to work on a new project, some new (or old) health problem pops up to interfere.

If that's the case, you may ask, why do I persist in attempting to work? Why not just sit back, cash my disability check, and not worry about trying to work? The fact is that, as the title of this book says, "I'd (really, really) rather be working." And that is for two important reasons: I need the money that the income from writing brings me, and I get a great deal of satisfaction from the act of writing my books and from the fact that they help others.

I wrote *When Muscle Pain Won't Go Away* because I wanted to know more about fibromyalgia. I can still remember the moment when I realized that it might have an impact on others. The thought scared me, almost enough for me to back off. However, at that time, I had no regular income; my VA check was around $500 and there was no way I could survive on that. So I moved ahead with the book. I am still in shock when I think about a lifetime sales of around 60,000 copies by the fall of 2001. I feel that in spite of my health problems, I managed to help some other people cope with the problems caused by fibromyalgia. And now I hope that this book will also help people manage financially and find the work that is best suited for them.

There is something that everyone can do at whatever level of limitation he or she has. Remember, as I've said more than once in this book, you may have very few limitations or you may have more. Depending upon your own personal knowledge, skills, and interests, you may be able to generate enough money to be financially comfortable or just enough to contribute to your income in a more limited amount. There is something that you can do, if you are willing to take the time to find it.

As for myself, I have been a nonfiction writer for thirty-five years, but I dream of writing fiction as well. I've completed several novels, received some nice feedback on them, but I haven't sold one yet. I intend to keep trying on that as well. Writing fiction is difficult, but it is also wonderful to watch characters develop and take life.

The point is that I do some work, but I also do something else with my life, something I would recommend to anyone, but especially to someone who is unable to work even a little. I volunteer. Find a place and a cause that matters to you and offer to volunteer. While it won't bring you any money, it will bring you a sense of purpose and the knowledge that you have something to give back to the world you live in. There is also the chance that someday the experience you gain in volunteering may become enough to bring in some money. Don't make that the primary reason you volunteer; just don't lose sight of the fact that it may help in the future.

In 1993, I went through the Denton Citizens Police Academy program for community members because I wanted to learn more about police departments and police officers for my fiction writing. Instead, I found myself involved in the department, caring about the police officers in a way that I hadn't expected. I was fairly typical in that my only exposure to police officers was as the result of a couple of minor accidents in the 1970s and two speeding tickets in 1980. My initial reaction to a police squad car when I was driving was to check my speedometer or to see if I was doing anything wrong. Now when I see one, I'm more likely to honk or wave or see if the officer needs help.

Over the years since 1993, as a member of the CPA Alumni Association, I have helped select a number of Officers of the Year, helped raise money for one officer who had a serious illness and another one whose baby had to have heart surgery not long after birth, and baby-sat when the officers needed someone to watch children until either a family member or Child Protective Services could pick them up. I've sent cards on behalf of the group to several of the officers who had to work a very rough automobile wreck, upon their retirement, or after the death of a family member, and helped provide food and serve it at our annual Officers' Appreciation Day. I know many of the officers, and I've come to feel a part of the department. I have served as an officer several times in the Alumni organization and would like to serve as president, but I know that my health wouldn't allow me to put in that much work.

I know there are many people who volunteer for many worthwhile organizations and causes and, since the September 11, 2001, terrorist attacks, volunteering has taken on a new life in our country. I urge you to find something. Become active in an organization such as the Red Cross, the American Cancer Society, or an animal rescue group, or attend a citizens' police or fire academy and then join the alumni association afterward to provide help. While thousands of Americans have been volunteering for years, it has recently become more visible. If you are uncertain of local opportunities or need help finding a place to volunteer, the federal government is making it easier than ever to find such opportunities, on a local basis or on a wider scale. Go to www.firstgov.gov, and under the "Citizens" column, click on "Volunteer." You will be directed to a number of Web sites, including not only the familiar "Peace Corps" but also newer groups that have been established or revamped in response to September 11. You can search for an opportunity geographically (within a specified number of miles of where you live) and use other options. Not every local group has signed up with these sites, but more are being continually added.

There are so many needs out there where volunteering can make a difference. It will make a difference not only for those you help, but it will make a difference for you. Some of the organizations need people who can give a certain number of hours a week at a set time or place. I know that I can't predict when I will be able to get out and do something because of my fibromyalgia. So I have taken on tasks that I can handle at my own pace, generally at home, but sometimes at the police department.

For a writer, I am having a hard time explaining why this means so much to me. I have had some of my alumni and police officer friends tell me to slow down, or ask why I insist on doing something that quite often leaves me exhausted. I do it because I am giving something back to the world and to my community. It gives me a sense of belonging as well as service. I've never wanted to be a police officer—the thought never occurred to me—but now I see what they do every day, and how they make Denton a safe place to live. By helping them, I am helping the city at large, and I am being productive, which adds to my feelings of self-worth. I hope the time never comes when I can't do at least some little thing to help out.

I've written this book because I want others with chronic illnesses to know they can still work. You may only need to change the way you work or you may have to make bigger changes. It may not be at the job or career that you had before your illness struck, but it can still be meaningful and, for most of you, it can go a long way toward providing you not only some financial security, but also that sense of satisfaction of being a productive human being. You can do something and sometimes the return you get, financially or emotionally, may not even be in direct proportion to the level of physical work you do. Use your mind when your body rebels.

I wish you well in your search for work, either for someone else or on your own. Let me know how you have managed by writing to me in care of AMACOM or at gbackstrom@verizonmail.com. Good luck!

Gayle Backstrom

Appendix A

Resources

In writing a book such as this one, I have two goals. First, I want to provide you, the reader, with a solid foundation in the body of the book. Second, I want to provide you with a direction in which to search for material that will allow you to continue the process.

Under publications I have assembled material from my own research as well as from some of the materials recommended on government and nonprofit organizations' Web sites. I have tried to include only those resources that are in print. However, there is always a chance that the status of a publication may change between the time I write this and the time you read it.

I know that it would be very expensive for you to attempt to purchase every one of these publications. You can, however, go to your local library for most of them, even if you must request them through interlibrary loan. Another way for you to evaluate which ones you might want to own personally is to visit a bookstore such as Barnes & Noble or Borders and look them over. Also, now that Amazon.com is including pages from the books it sells, you may be able to do all of this online in case you can't get to one of the larger bookstores. Good luck and good reading.

Publications

Abrams, Rhonda. *The Successful Business Plan: Secrets and Strategies*, 3rd ed. Palo Alto, Calif.: Running R Media, 2000.

Albert, Susan Wittig. *Writing from Life: Telling Your Soul's Story*. New York: Jeremy P. Tarcher/Putnam, 1997.

Alliance for Technology Access. *Computer and Web Resources for People with Disabilities,* 3rd ed. Alameda, Calif.: Hunter House, 2000.

Allon, Janet. *The Business of Bliss: How to Profit from Doing What You Love*. New York: Hearst Books, 1999.

Anderson, Sandy. *The Work-at-Home Balancing Act: The Professional Resource Guide for Managing Yourself, Your Work, and Your Family at Home*. New York: Avon, 1998.

Applegate, Jane. *201 Great Ideas for Your Small Business*. Princeton, N.J.: Bloomberg Press, 1998. (Look for revised edition due in June 2002.)

Arden, Lynie. *The Work at Home Sourcebook,* 7th ed. Boulder, Colo.: Live Oak Publications, 1999.

Arena, Barbara. *The Complete Idiot's Guide to Making Money with Your Hobby*. Indianapolis: National Crafts Association, Alpha Books, 2001.

Attard, Janet. *The Home Office and Small Business Answer Book: Solutions to the Most Frequently Asked Questions About Starting and Running Your Business,* 2nd ed. New York: Owl Books, 2000.

Backstrom, Gayle, and Bernard Rubin. *When Muscle Pain Won't Go Away,* 3rd ed. Dallas: Taylor Publishing, 1998.

Bangs, David H. Jr., *The Business Planning Guide: Creating a Plan for Success in Your Own Business,* 8th ed. Chicago: Upstart Publishing, 1998.

Bangs, David H. Jr., and Andi Axman. *Work at Home Wisdom: A Collection of Quips, Tips, and Inspirations to Balance Work, Family, and Home*. Chicago: Upstart Publishing, 1998.

Bear, John B., and Mariah P. Bear. *Bears' Guide to Earning Degrees by Distance Learning*. Berkeley, Calif.: Ten Speed Press, 2001.

Benson, Herbert, and Miriam Z. Klipper, contributor. *The Relaxation Response*. New York: HarperCollins, 2000.

Benson, Herbert, and William Proctor. *Beyond the Relaxation Response: How to Harness the Healing Power of Your Personal Beliefs*. New York: Berkley Group, 1994.

Bickham, Jack M. *Writing and Selling Your Novel.* Cincinnati: Writer's Digest Books, 1996.

Billington, Dottie. *Life Is an Attitude: How to Grow Forever Better,* 2nd ed. Sammamish, Wash.: Lowell Leigh Books, 2001.

Bond, W. J. *Going Solo: Developing a Home-Based Consulting Business from the Ground Up.* New York: McGraw-Hill Professional Publishing, 1997.

Boyd, Margaret A. *Crafts Supply Source Book: The Comprehensive Shop-by-Mail Guide for Thousands of Craft Materials,* 5th ed. Cincinnati: Betterway Books, 1999.

Brabec, Barbara. *The Crafts Business Answer Book and Resource Guide.* New York: M. Evans & Co, 1998.

———. *Creative Cash: How to Profit from Your Special Artistry, Creativity, Hand Skills and Related Knowhow.* Roseville, Calif.: Prima Publishing, 1998.

———. *Handmade for Profit: Hundreds of Secrets to Success in Selling Arts & Crafts.* New York: M. Evans & Co., 1996.

———. *Make It Profitable! How to Make Your Art, Craft, Design, Writing, or Publishing Business More Efficient, More Satisfying, and More Profitable.* New York: M. Evans & Co., 2000.

Branden, Nathaniel, *How to Raise Your Self-Esteem,* reissue ed. New York: Bantam Books, 1988.

———. *The Power of Self-Esteem: An Inspiring Look at Our Most Important Psychological Resource.* Deerfield Beach, Fla.: Health Communications, 1992.

Bredin, A. *The Home Office Solution: How to Balance Your Professional and Personal Lives While Working from Home.* New York: John Wiley & Sons, 1998.

———. *The Virtual Office Survival Handbook: What Telecommuters and Entrepreneurs Need to Succeed in Today's Nontraditional Workplace.* New York: John Wiley & Sons, 1996.

Bucy, Douglas R., and Rebecca A. Nolan. *Help Yourself: Problem Solving for the Disabled.* New York: Macmillan General Reference, 1996.

Burstiner, Irwin. *The Small Business Handbook: A Comprehensive Guide to Starting and Running Your Own Business,* 3rd ed. New York: Fireside, 1997.

Cameron, Julia. *The Artist's Way: A Spiritual Path to Higher Creativity.* New York: Jeremy P. Tarcher/Putnam, 1992.

————. *The Vein of Gold: A Journey to Your Creative Heart.* New York: Jeremy P. Tarcher/Putnam, 1997.

Canfield, Jack, Mark Victor Hansen, and Les Hewitt. *The Power of Focus.* Deerfield Beach, Fla.: Health Communications, 2000.

Carlson, Richard. *Don't Sweat the Small Stuff, and It's All Small Stuff.* New York: Hyperion, 1997.

Carlson, Richard, and Wayne Dyer. *You Can Be Happy No Matter What: Five Principles Your Therapist Never Told You,* Novato, Calif.: New World Library, 1997.

Carter, Gary. *J.K. Lasser's Taxes Made Easy for Your Home-Based Business: The Ultimate Tax Handbook for Self-Employed Professional, Consultants, and Freelancers.* New York: John Wiley & Sons, 2000. (Updated annually.)

Cobe, Patricia, and Ellen H. Parlapiano. *Mompreneurs: A Mother's Practical Guide to Work at Home Success.* New York: Berkley, 1996.

————. *Mompreneurs Online: Using the Internet to Build Work@Home Success.* New York: Perigee, 2001.

Cook, Mel. *Home Business, Big Business: The Definitive Guide to Starting and Operating On-Line and Traditional Home-Based Ventures.* San Francisco: Jossey Bass, 1998.

Covey, Stephen R. *Daily Reflections for Highly Effective People: Living the 7 Habits of Highly Effective People Every Day.* New York: Fireside, 1994.

————. *The 7 Habits of Highly Effective People.* New York: Simon & Schuster, 1990.

Davidson, Jeff. *The Complete Idiot's Guide to Reaching Your Goals.* New York: Alpha Books, 1998.

Davis, Will. *Start Your Own Business for $1,000 or Less.* Chicago: Upstart Publishing, 1995.

Dietz, Janis. *Yes, You Can!!! Go Beyond Physical Adversity and Live Life to Its Fullest.* New York: Demos Medical Publishing (SCB International), 2000.

Dorian, J. S. *Above and Beyond: 365 Meditations for Transcending Chronic Pain and Illness.* New York: Plume, 1996.

Doyle, Alice Weiss. *No More Job Interviews: Self-Employment Strategies for People with Disabilities.* St. Petersburg, Fla.: Training Resource Network, 2000. www.trninc.com/nomoreinterviews.htm

Edwards, Paul and Sarah Edwards. *The Best Home Businesses for the 21st Century,* 3rd ed. New York: Jeremy P. Tarcher/Putnam, 1999.

———. *Finding Your Perfect Work: The New Career Guide to Making a Living, Creating a Life.* New York: Jeremy P. Tarcher/Putnam, 1996.

———. *Getting Business to Come to You: A Complete Do-It-Yourself Guide to Attracting All the Business You Can Enjoy,* 2nd ed., New York: Jeremy P. Tarcher/Putnam, 1998.

———. *Home-Based Business for Dummies.* Foster City, Calif.: IDG Books, 2000.

———. *Making Money in Cyberspace: The Inside Information You Need to Start or Take Your Own Business On-Line.* New York: Jeremy P. Tarcher/Putnam, 1998.

———. *Secrets of Self-Employment: Surviving and Thriving on the Ups and Downs of Being Your Own Boss.* New York: Jeremy P. Tarcher/Putnam, 1996.

———. *Working from Home: Everything You Need to Know About Living and Working Under the Same Roof,* 5th ed. New York: Jeremy P. Tarcher/Putnam, 1999.

Folger, Liz. *The Stay-at-Home Mom's Guide to Making Money from Home,* rev. 2nd ed. Roseville, Calif.: Prima Publishing, 2000.

Frazier, Shirley George. *How to Start a Home-Based Gift Basket Business.* Guilford, Conn.: Globe Pequot Press, 2000.

Gilkerson, Linda, and Theresia Paauwe. *Self-Employment: From Dream to Reality.* Indianapolis: JIST Works, 1997.

Gleek, Fred. *Marketing and Promoting Your Own Seminars and Workshops.* Henderson, Nev.: Fast Forward Press, 2001.

―――. *Publishing for Maximum Profit: A Step by Step Guide to Making Big Money with Your Book and Other How To Material.* Henderson, Nev.: Fast Forward Press, 2001.

Glink, Ilyce R. *50 Simple Things You Can Do to Improve Your Personal Finances: How to Spend Less, Save More, and Make the Most of What You Have.* New York: Three Rivers Press, 2001.

Jeffers, Susan. *Feel the Fear and Beyond: Mastering the Techniques for Doing It Anyway.* New York: Random House, 1998.

―――. *Feel the Fear and Do It Anyway*, reissue ed. New York: Fawcett Columbine, 1992.

Jones, Katina. *Adams Businesses You Can Start Almanac.* Holbrook, Mass.: Adams Media, 1996.

Kabat-Zinn, Jon. *Full Catastrophe Living: Using the Wisdom of Your Body and Mind to Face Stress, Pain, and Illness* (The Program of the Stress Reduction Clinic at the University of Massachusetts Medical Center). New York: Delta Books, 1990.

Kanarek, Lisa. *Home Office Life: Making a Space to Work at Home.* Gloucester, Mass.: Rockport Publishers, 2001.

―――. *101 Home Office Success Secrets*, 2nd ed. Franklin Lakes, N.J.: Career Press, 2000.

―――. *Organizing Your Home Office for Success: Expert Strategies That Work for You.* Dallas: Blakely Press, 1998.

Keirsey, David. *Please Understand Me II, Temperament, Character, and Intelligence.* Del Mar, Calif.: Prometheus Nemesis Book Co., 1998.

Kelly, Jason. *The Neatest Little Guide to Making Money Online.* New York: Plume, 2000.

King, Stephen. *On Writing: A Memoir of the Craft.* New York: Pocket Books, 2001.

Lee, Andrew, Andy Lee, and Jim Hightower. *Backyard Market Gardening: The Entrepreneur's Guide to Selling What You Grow.* Buena Vista, Calif.: Good Earth Publications, 1995.

Lehmkuhl, Dorothy, and Dolores Cotter Lamping. *Organizing for the Creative Person.* New York: Crown, 1994.

Littman, Barbara. *The Women's Business Resource Guide,* 2nd ed. Chicago: Contemporary Books, 1996.

Lonier, Terri. *Working Solo,* 2nd ed. New York: John Wiley & Sons, 1998.

McGrath, Jinks. *The Encyclopedia of Jewelry-Making Techniques.* Philadelphia: Running Press, 1995.

McMeekin, Gail. *The 12 Secrets of Highly Creative Women: A Portable Mentor.* New York: MJF Books, Fine Communications, 2000.

Melnik, Jan, *How to Start a Home-Based Secretarial Services Business.* Guilford, Conn.: Globe Pequot Press, 1999.

Misner, Ivan R., and Don Morgan. *Masters of Networking: Building Relationships for Your Pocketbook and Soul.* Marietta, Ga.: Bard Press, 2000.

Oberrecht, Ken, and Paula Brisco, eds. *How to Start a Home-Based Craft Business,* 3rd ed. Guilford, Conn.: Globe Pequot Press, 2000.

Parker, Lucy. *How to Start a Home-Based Writing Business,* 3rd ed. Revised and updated by Karen Ivory. Guilford, Conn.: The Globe Pequot Press, 2000.

Poynter, Dan. *The Self-Publishing Manual: How to Write, Print and Sell Your Own Book,* 13th ed. Santa Barbara, Calif.: Para Publishing, 2001.

———. *Writing Nonfiction: Turning Thoughts into Books.* Santa Barbara, Calif.: Para Publishing, 2000.

Price, Stanley J. Jr., and Stanley Price. *Cleaning Up Making Money.* SJ Associates, 2000.

Pullen, M. C. *You Can Make Money from Your Hobby: Building a Business Doing What You Love.* Nashville: Broadman & Holman Publishers, 1999.

Register, Cheri. *The Chronic Illness Experience: Embracing the Imperfect Life.* Revised edition of *Living with Chronic Illness: Days of Patience and Passion.* Center City, Minn.: Hazelton Information Education, 1999.

Ross, Tom and Marilyn Ross. *The Complete Guide to Self-Publishing,* 3rd ed. Cincinnati: Writer's Digest Books, 1995.

Shaw, Lisa. *How to Make Money Publishing from Home,* rev. 2nd ed. Rocklin, Calif.: Prima Publishing, 2000.

Stine, Jean Marie. *Writing Successful Self-Help & How-To Books.* New York: John Wiley & Sons, 1997.

St. James, Elaine. *Simplify Your Life: 100 Ways to Slow Down and Enjoy the Things That Really Matter.* New York: Hyperion, 1994.

———. *Inner Simplicity: 100 Ways to Regain Peace and Nourish Your Soul.* New York: Hyperion, 1995.

Swain, Dwight. *Techniques of the Selling Writer.* Oklahoma City: University of Oklahoma Press, 1982.

Tieger, Paul D., and Barbara Barron-Tieger. *Do What You Are: Discover the Perfect Career for You Through the Secrets of Personality Type.* Boston: Little, Brown, 1992.

Vogler, Christopher. *The Writer's Journey: Mythic Structure for Storytellers & Screenwriters,* 2nd ed. Studio City, Calif.: Michael Wiese Productions, 1998.

Von Oech, Roger. *A Whack on the Side of the Head: How You Can Be More Creative,* rev. ed. New York: Warner Books, 1998.

Weddle, Peter D. *Weddle's Job-Seeker's Guide to Employment Web Sites 2001.* New York: AMACOM Books, 2000.

West, Janice. *Marketing Your Arts & Crafts: Creative Ways to Profit from Your Work.* Fort Worth: The Summit Group, 1994.

Westberg, Granger. *Good Grief: A Constructive Approach to the Problem of Loss,* 35th ed. Philadelphia: Augsburg Fortress Pubs., 1983.

Winter, Barbara J. *Making a Living Without a Job: Winning Ways for Creating Work That You Love.* New York: Bantam, 1993.

Zelinski, Ernie J. *The Joy of Not Working: A Book for the Retired, Unemployed, and Overworked,* 3rd ed. Berkeley, Calif.: Ten Speed Press, 1997.

Department of Labor: Office of Disability Employment Policy

1331 F Street, N.W., Suite 300
Washington, DC 20004
Voice: (202) 376-6200
TTY: (202) 376-6205
Fax: (202) 376-6219
http://www.dol.gov/dol/odep/

The Web site will provide you with links to programs and services, the library, technical assistance materials, the Job Accommodation Network, the Small Business and Self-Employment Service, as well job links, state liaisons, and more.

Job Accommodation Network

The Job Accommodation Network (JAN) is a toll-free consulting service of the U.S. Department of Labor's Office of Disability Employment Policy. JAN provides information to anyone on workplace accommodations and on the employment provisions of the Americans with Disabilities Act (ADA). Service is available via a toll-free number: 1-800-ADA-WORK (1-800-232-9675) or 1-800-526-7234. In addition, a Searchable Online Accommodation Resource (SOAR) is available on JAN's Web site: http://www.jan.wvu.edu/english/homeus.htm. Also, go to http://www.jan.wvu.edu/links for an extensive list of more outstanding resources, including information on specific chronic illnesses and disabilities.

Small Business and Self-Employment Service

The Small Business and Self-Employment Service (SBSES) is staffed by the Job Accommodation Network and can be contacted at:

P.O. Box 6080
Morgantown, WV 26506-6080
Voice/TT: (800) 526-7234
Fax: (304) 293-5407
http://www.jan.wvu.edu/SBSES
E-mail: kcording@wvu.edu

Telephones are answered Monday through Thursday from 8:00 A.M. to 8:00 P.M. and Friday from 8:00 A.M. to 7:00 P.M. (Eastern time). Voice mail records messages after hours, weekends, and holidays. The SBSES has extensive links and contact information at the following Web site: http://www.jan.wvu.edu/SBSES/TABLEOFCONTENTS.HTM

U.S. Small Business Administration and Related Resources

The U.S. Small Business Administration (SBA) is dedicated to providing quality customer-oriented, full-service programs, and accurate, timely information to the entrepreneurial community. The SBA provides financial assistance in the form of loan guarantees rather than direct loans. The SBA does not provide grants to start or expand a business. The SBA provides an extensive presence on the Internet, and it is worthwhile to investigate its many programs and services.

Small Business Administration
409 Third Street, S.W., Suite 7600
Washington, DC 20416
Voice: (202) 205-6744
Fax: (202) 205-7064
TDD: (202) 344-6640
SBA Answer Desk: (800) U-ASK-SBA
http://www.sba.gov

Government Contracting and Business Development

"Our job at SBA is to help small, disadvantaged, and women-owned businesses build their potential to compete more successfully in our global economy. We strive to be the premier source of information and procurement assistance for our customers."

http://www.sba.gov/gcbd/

Office of Veteran's Affairs Small Business Administration

Fosters enhanced entrepreneurship among eligible veterans by providing increased opportunities.

http://www.sba.gov/VETS/

Department of Veterans Affairs VETBIZ: The Veteran Business Portal for the Federal Government

http://www.vetbiz.gov/

Office of Women's Business Ownership

The U.S. SBA is doing more than ever to help level the playing field for women entrepreneurs, who still face unique obstacles in the world of business. The SBA's Office of Women's Business Ownership (OWBO) is leading the way. With a network of women's business owner representatives in every district office, more than one hundred mentoring roundtables and women-owned venture capital companies, nearly seventy women's business centers in forty states, and the Online Women's Business Center on the Internet, OWBO is helping women start and build successful businesses.

Voice: (202) 205-6673
http://www.sba.gov/womeninbusiness/

Small Business Development Centers

The U.S SBA administers the Small Business Development Center (SBDC) Program to provide management assistance to current and prospective small business owners.

SBDCs offer one-stop assistance to small businesses by providing a wide variety of information and guidance in central and easily accessible branch locations. The program is a cooperative effort of the private sector; the educational community; and federal, state and local governments. It enhances economic development by providing small businesses with management and technical assistance. SBDCs also make special efforts to reach minority members of socially and economically disadvantaged groups, veterans, women, and people with disabilities.

Assistance is provided to both current and potential small business owners. SBDCs also provide assistance to small businesses applying for Small Business Innovation and Research grants from federal agencies.

http://www.sba.gov/regions/states.html

Office of Native American Affairs

"The Office of Native American Affairs is dedicated to ensuring that American Indians, Native Alaskans, and Native Hawaiians seeking to create, develop, and expand small businesses have full access to the necessary business development and expansion tools available through the Agency's entrepreneurial development, lending and procurement programs. Additionally, ONAA administers the Tribal Business Information Centers project designed to offer culturally-

tailored business development assistance to Native American entrepreneurs."

> http://www.sba.gov/naa/

Tribal Business Information Centers

To address the unique conditions encountered by reservation-based
Native Americans in their efforts to create, develop, and expand
small businesses, the SBA has funded the Tribal Business Information
Centers (TBICs) project. The project is designed to provide culturally
tailored business development assistance to prospective and current
small business owners. TBICs, a partnership arrangement between a
tribe or tribal college and the SBA, offer access to a wide variety of
resources and practical guidance at accessible reservation locations.

> http://www.sba.gov/naa/tribes/#tbics

Financing Your Business

> http://www.sba.gov/financing/

The Service Corps of Retired Executives

The SCORE Association (Service Corps of Retired Executives
[SCORE]) is a nonprofit association dedicated to entrepreneur education and the formation, growth, and success of small business nationwide.

SCORE is a resource partner with the SBA. SCORE Association
volunteers serve as "Counselors to America's Small Business." Working and retired executives and business owners donate their time and
expertise as volunteer business counselors and provide confidential
counseling and mentoring free of charge.

> 409 Third Street, S.W.
> Washington, DC 20024
> Voice: (800) 634-0245
> http://www.score.org/

Online Women's Business Center

The Online Women's Business Center provides business resources
and related links for women at the following Web site:

> http://www.onlinewbc.org/

SBDC National Information Clearinghouse

"Facilitates the sharing and exchange of information among Small Business Development Centers, the Small Business Administration, and other business-oriented contacts."

SBDC National Information Clearinghouse
145 Duncan Dr., Suite 200
San Antonio, TX 78226
Voice: (800) 689-1912
Fax: (210) 458-7840
E-mail: sbdcnet@utsa.edu
http://sbdcnet.utsa.edu

The Small Business Classroom

The Small Business Classroom is an online resource for training and informing entrepreneurs and other students of enterprise. It is a new, easy-to-use dimension in entrepreneurial training.

http://www.classroom.sba.gov/

BusinessLINC

"In previous business-to-business relationship programs, the relationship between the large company and small business was referred to as mentor-protégé programs. The BusinessLINC Protégé Network is a comprehensive online database that provides immediate registration for both protégé opportunities and small business procurement/contracting opportunities through SBA's PRO-Net system. Protégé registration is hyperlinked to PRO-Net so that your information can efficiently be included in small business profiles scanned by large businesses for both mentor-protégé relationships and small business contracting opportunities."

http://www.businesslinc.sba.gov/

Small Business Administration Hotlist

This highly recommended site contains an extensive list of links related to all aspects of small business development. There is also a section specifically targeting home business resources.

http://www.sbaonline.sba.gov/hotlist/

Social Security Administration

Office of Public Inquiries
6401 Security Boulevard

Room 4-C-5 Annex
Baltimore, MD 21235-6401
Voice: (800) 772-1213
TTY: (800) 325-0778
http://www.ssa.gov/

Selected Social Security Web Sites

Office Locator

https://s3abaca.ssa.gov/pro/fol/fol-home.html

Disability Program Information

http://www.ssa.gov/disability/

Employment Support Programs
Includes information on work incentive programs such as PASS

http://www.ssa.gov/work/

2001 Red Book on Employment Support

http://www.ssa.gov/work/ResourcesToolkit/redbook.html

Questions and Answers on Extended Medicare Coverage for Working People with Disabilities

http://www.ssa.gov/work/ResourcesToolkit/Health/qaextendcare.htm

Montana University Affiliated Rural Institute on Disabilities
Provides information on PASS plans.

http://www.passplan.org

The Work Site
The Work Site is sponsored by the Social Security Administration, Office of Employment Support Programs. "Our Mission is to promote the employment of Social Security beneficiaries with disabilities by: designing policies that make work pay; promoting research and program innovation; educating the public about programs and services that facilitate entry into the workforce; and partnering with

other public and private groups to remove employment barriers for
people with disabilities."

> http://www.ssa.gov/work/

Social Security Online: Representing Clients

> http://www.ssa.gov/representation/

National Organization of Social Security Claimants' Representatives

"The National Organization of Social Security Claimants' Representatives (NOSSCR) is committed to providing the highest quality rep-
resentation and advocacy on behalf of persons who are seeking Social
Security and Supplemental Security Income."

> 6 Prospect Street
> Midland Park, NJ 07432-1691
> Voice: (800) 431-2804
> E-mail: nosscr@worldnet.att.net
> http://www.nosscr.org/

The Rural Institute, University of Montana

Publishes the book *It Doesn't Take a Rocket Scientist to Understand &
Use Social Security Work Incentives: A Manual for Social Security Work
Incentives Training,* 5th ed.

> The Rural Institute
> Adult Community Services and Supports Department
> 52 Corbin Hall
> The University of Montana
> Missoula, MT 59812
> Voice (toll-free): (877) 243-2476
> http://www.ruralinstitute.umt.edu/training/other/RocketScience/
>   RS_Cover.htm

State Economic Development Resources

The listings on the following Web site represent a variety of state
resources related to economic development and growing a small or
home-based business. It is worthwhile to spend some time on the
Web site(s) for your state. Many have regional funding programs

listed as well as links to resources related to business development at local, state, national, and international levels.

http://www.jan.wvu.edu/SBSES/ECONOMICDEVELOPMENT.HTM

Associations and Organizations

The SBSES also gives a long list of associations and organizations. I have included just five to give you a feeling for what is available. For the complete list, go to this Web site: http://www.jan.wvu.edu/ SBSES/ASSOCIATIONSANDORGANIZATIONS.HTM

American Association of Home-Based Business

A nonprofit organization providing information for those who run a business from their home.

P.O. Box 10023
Rockville, MD 20849
Voice: (800) 447-9710
Fax: (301) 963-7042
E-mail: aahbb@crosslink.net
http://www.aahbb.org

Mountain Microenterprise Fund

Mountain Microenterprise Fund (MMF) is a nonprofit organization that helps create and sustain jobs by enabling low- to moderate-income people of western North Carolina who are unable to secure traditional loans (because they do not have sufficient business experience, a good credit history, or collateral) to start or expand economically viable microbusinesses.

MMF helps individuals develop basic business skills, network with other businesses, access MMF's small business loan pool, and increase their self-confidence and thus their chances of business success.

Contact Person: Greg Walker-Wilson
Economic Development
29 1/2 Page Avenue
Asheville, NC 28801
Toll free: (888) 389-3089
Voice: (828) 253-2834

Fax: (828) 255-7953
E-mail: MMF@mtnmicro.org
http://mtnmicro.org/

National Federation of Independent Business

NFIB, the National Federation of Independent Business, is the largest advocacy organization representing small and independent businesses in Washington, D.C. and all fifty state capitals.

53 Century Boulevard, Suite 300
Nashville, TN 37214
Toll free: (800) NFIB-NOW
Voice: (615) 872-5300
E-mail: sales@nfibonline.com
http://www.nfib.com

Network for Entrepreneurs with Disabilities

This site is of interest to entrepreneurs. It includes links to some really good resources on the Internet and is ideally suited for small and/or home-based businesses, those considering entrepreneurship, and especially persons with disabilities involved in or interested in entrepreneurship.

Canada/Nova Scotia Business Service Centre
1575 Brunswick Street
Halifax, NS B3J 2G1
Canada
Voice/TTY: (902) 426-0561
Fax: (902) 461-9484
E-mail: newd@cbsc.ic.gc.ca
http://www.entrepreneurdisability.org/

United States Chamber of Commerce

1615 H Street, N.W.
Washington, D.C. 20062
Voice: 202-659-6000
Fax: 202-463-3190
E-mail: smallbiz@uschamber.com
http://www.uschamber.org

Vocational Rehabilitation State Offices

By contacting your local vocational rehabilitation office, you will tap into a wealth of resources related to employment options for people with disabilities. Vocational rehabilitation offices are state-supported services that assist individuals with disabilities who are pursuing meaningful careers, as I discussed in Chapter 8. Rather than listing each state's offices, I recommend that you go to your state's Web site and follow the links to obtain specific information on those services offered.

For example, for the state of Texas, the Web site is located at http://www.state.tx.us. From the menu on the left side of the screen, select "Health and Family Services," and then under that click on "Disability Services." You will have a choice of several departments including "Rehabilitation Services." By clicking on that link, you will arrive at http://www.rehab.state.tx.us/services.htm.

In the state of Michigan, go to http://www.michigan.gov/mdcd and click on "Disability and Rehabilitation" on the left side of the screen. The Disability and Rehabilitation site will offer you choices from the Michigan Rehabilitation Services (MRS) to disability legislation.

Click on Michigan Rehabilitation Services and you will find information on how to obtain help in working either for yourself or for someone else, plus a great deal more information and related links.

Additional Disability and Small Business Web Sites

Here are a few examples of what you can find.

Disability Resources

"Disability Resources, inc. is a nonprofit 501(c)(3) organization established to promote and improve awareness, availability and accessibility of information that can help people with disabilities live, learn, love, work and play independently."

http://www.disabilityresources.org/

Americans with Disabilities Act Document Center

This Web site contains copies of the Americans with Disabilities Act of 1990 (ADA), ADA regulations, technical assistance manuals prepared by the United States Equal Employment Opportunity Commission (EEOC) and the United States Department of Justice (DOJ), and technical assistance documents sponsored by the National Institute on Disability and Rehabilitation Research (NIDRR) and reviewed by EEOC or DOJ.

> http://www.jan.wvu.edu/kinder/

The Catalog of Federal Domestic Assistance
A governmentwide compendium of federal programs, projects, services, and activities that provides assistance or benefits to the American public. It contains financial and nonfinancial assistance programs administered by departments and establishments of the federal government.

> Federal Domestic Assistance Catalog Staff (MVS)
> General Services Administration
> Voice: (202) 708-5126
> Toll-free answering service: (800) 669-8331
> http://www.cfda.gov/

Consumer Protection Resources

Better Business Bureau
"Our mission is to promote and foster the highest ethical relationship between businesses and the public." You can find links to find a local Better Business Bureau office or find helpful information for consumer guidance in areas such as how to detect scams.

> Council of Better Business Bureaus, Inc.
> 4200 Wilson Boulevard, Suite 800
> Arlington, VA 22203-1804
> Voice: (703) 276-0100
> Fax: (703) 525-8277
> http://www.bbb.org/

Federal Trade Commission, Bureau of Consumer Protection
> Consumer toll-free line: (877) FTC-HELP
> http://www.ftc.gov

National Foundation for Credit Counseling
For help, contact the national toll-free crisis hotline at 1-800-388-2227, to locate the member agency in your area or receive online

counseling. The Web site has a list of local organizations. "NFCC is a national network of 1,450 nonprofit member agencies. Learn about our full range of services, from accredited money management education to confidential budget, credit and debt counseling, and debt repayment plans, to home-buyer education, and mortgage programs."

http://www.nfcc.org/

State, County, and City Government Consumer Protection Offices

"City, county and state consumer protection offices provide consumers with important services. They mediate complaints, conduct investigations, prosecute offenders of consumer laws, license and regulate a variety of professionals, promote strong consumer protection legislation, provide educational materials and advocate in the consumer interest."

http://www.pueblo.gsa.gov/crh/state.htm

Consumer World

Links to almost every consumer agency you can think of throughout the world including the attorney general's offices for each state.

http://www.consumerworld.org/pages/agencies.htm

United States Consumer Gateway

The U.S. Consumer Gateway—"consumer.gov"—is a "one-stop" link to a broad range of federal information resources available online.

http://www.consumer.gov/

Appendix B

Assistive Technology

According to the Assistive Technology Act of 1998, assistive technology is "any item, piece of equipment, or product system, whether acquired commercially, modified, or customized, that is used to increase, maintain, or improve the functional capabilities of individuals with disabilities." The term assistive technology, in its broadest sense, can mean almost anything that can be used to enable an individual to perform any activity of daily living by allowing him or her to overcome the limitations imposed by a disability or chronic illness.

So it could apply to a wide range of devices, from the cane to assist someone in walking to the sophisticated communications equipment that physicist Stephen Hawking, who has Lou Gehrig's disease (amyotrophic lateral sclerosis). He uses a speech synthesizer, a small portable computer, and a software program called "Equalizer." This equipment not only allows him to communicate with those around him, but has also enabled him to write scientific papers and give speeches at scientific conferences.

While most of the people who will read this book will not require such sophisticated technology, there are still many options that can assist them in working. As part of the U.S. Department of Education, the National Institute on Disability and Rehabilitation Research supports research, including in technology, which will improve the lives of those facing disability. ABLEDATA (http://www.abledata. com) was named to Forbes.com's "Best of the Web" for its information on assistive technology.

197

Another way to find information on products, availability, cost, and financial assistance for purchasing assistive devices is to go to the Job Accommodation Network Web site (http://www.jan.wvu.edu/links) and click on "information providers" or "technology-related resources."

Appendix C

Personal Stories

I wanted to include information from others who face problems in working because of their chronic illnesses, so I went online to several forums and groups. I asked those who responded to my request to complete a questionnaire. Those stories follow. I give only the initials of the individuals to protect their privacy.

The purpose of the questionnaire was twofold: to learn about the problems they encountered, and to find out what they were doing to keep working, if anything. I have included only those questions that each person answered rather than repeating all of the questions each time.

A.'s Story

What is your chronic illness?

Osteoporosis with the subsequent lateral curvature of the spine, which throws my back muscles off balance.

How long have you had this illness?

I first discovered it in 1987 after raking leaves vigorously because I was in a hurry to get done. My back went out, but that was not the first time that happened. However, it was such severe pain and did not improve in the usual two weeks that I had to go to an orthopedic doctor, who found the condition through x-ray.

Are you employed?

No.

What is your occupation?

I was an R.N. Am writing fiction at present.

Have you changed your job because of your chronic illness?

I tried to find something that I could do that was less strenuous after I found out about the condition, but it was one frustration after another. I had worked for years in nursing homes and was not familiar with some other less strenuous forms of nursing. I also did not have a degree, which would have made it possible for me to get a better job. I worked on and off for the next eight years and finally decided it was time to retire.

Have you had to quit work because of your chronic illness?

Yes. As stated previously, after some frustrating tries.

Can you break your job into specific activities?

At present I am very busy with house chores as I will probably sell my house in the not so distant future. My husband died in March, and the house and grounds are too much for me. As a fiction writer I spend time sitting and typing, writing down information and brainstorming. With osteoporosis you are not supposed to sit for long periods of time and do need to do certain exercises, which I do. As a nursing home nurse the work was very physical and strenuous, required lifting, bending, pushing and pulling patients in bed, etc. I was told by the medical doctor not to lift over twenty-five pounds and it was quite impossible to continue working.

Do you consider yourself disabled?

No. I am able to do some jobs, only not the one which I was trained to do and which brought in some money for me.

Are you receiving any disability benefits?

No.

If you have changed jobs or reduced your working hours, how long ago did this happen?

This happened in 1987.

Has this improved your ability to work?

I am able to write with no problem, only I had never used a computer. I had to learn many new things. I am receiving social security now and hope to be able to continue going on without looking for a job.

Have you taken advantage of any vocational rehabilitation training?

No.

Have you told your employer about your chronic illness?

I had to at the time because I could not work and because in many cases they wanted me to be the only nurse in the facility. In case my back were to go out while working, this would be a very dangerous situation.

What was the response?

In most cases it meant that they did not want to hire me probably because of insurance reasons.

If you have not told your employer, what are your concerns about discussing your chronic illness?

It would usually mean they would not hire me, but I told them. As a writer I don't have a problem.

Have you used any assistive device, such as a cane, electric scooter, etc. for mobility?

Not so far. However, sometimes I was almost unable to get off the bed for quite a long period of time and then could hardly walk. Each time the back went out it was usually five to six weeks before I was back to normal. This also took a lot out of me physically. It was exhausting to have pain for a long period of time. And the pain was very severe at times. I would feel like I had aged ten years each time it happened.

Have you used anything to make doing your job any easier, such as an ergonomic computer keyboard, ergonomically designed office chair, voice recognition software?

No.

S.'s Story

What is your chronic illness? How long have you had it?

Fibromyalgia since 1999 and vertigo recurring from 1995.

Are you employed? What is your occupation?

Yes, senior clerk typist, but I have been off work for the last few months.

Have you changed your job because of your chronic illness? Have you had to quit work because of your chronic illness?

No. I am planning to go back to work. I don't know what else to do. I still have problems, but a lot of symptoms have been improved. Disability company is not paying me, and we don't have much money left.

Can you break your job into specific activities?

As senior clerk typist, I supervise a clerk, answer phones, direct customers at the counter, computer input, typing, payroll, xeroxing, filing, editing, log employee schedules in to the time book. My job is very fast paced and I have been shorthanded for over a year. It requires close-up reading/editing with numbers (payroll), typing and a lot of writing notes, order supplies, lift boxes and reorganize supply room by moving boxes to make room for next supply arrival and count tickets by hands, mostly using thumbs and index fingers, approximately few thousand a month.

I started out having tennis elbow to tendonitis. When I typed, my neck and right side of wrist and shoulder blade hurt so much. When I wrote, my hands and thumb and wrist hurt so much. My right-side wrist was swollen and I could not move it and I thought I sprained it. My doctor had me wear wrist braces for many months. I had spasms in my neck, backache and spasms in the back, so much pain on my shoulder and arms, and would have pain from my butt down to my right leg from sitting for long hours. I kept hurting my back from lifting boxes, started getting headache from stress, heartburn.

I started having bad allergies, infections, bad heartburn. Early afternoon I get so tired I drank three Mountain Dews to keep me going. Then I started having infection after infection, chronic fatigue, I took three weeks off but I had chronic fatigue, vertigo, and fibromyalgia and now I am off work.

Editing payroll every week hurt my eyes. Sometimes they would hurt for three days and I have to flip twelve pages of the time book back and forth until I input/edit approximately 160 employee schedules and their names are scattered all over the pages. My job requires me to sit in same position most of the day, causing neck, arm, and shoulder pain, spasm on my butt and pain down to my knee and leg.

My job requires me to use my hands all the time. Close-up reading/editing gives me headache and eye pain. My job requires alertness and concentration at all times. I have to answer to many people, meet due dates, make decisions, delegate, assist employee getting her job done, edit/correct payroll/paperwork mistakes that put me in a constant stress level. I had a hard time relaxing at work.

I no longer have brain fog, can think more clearly, but I noticed my thinking is not as sharp as it used to be a few months ago, and my reading comprehension is not as good as it used to be. I have been on all different [kinds of] medication and they have some effect on me. (Note: I didn't think I could go back to my old job with brain fog because my job requires me to memorize so many things. I now believe I can go back to work, but I am not as fast as I used to be. I have to work at my own pace even if that means I am going to get behind.)

Do you consider yourself disabled?

I am disabled right now. I have been treated for fibromyalgia since 1999 and disability insurance company didn't believe me back in 1999 and now they have not paid me, either.

Have you taken advantage of any vocational rehabilitation training?

No.

Have you told your employer about your chronic illness? What was the response?

I have been off work for three months. I have been telling my boss that I have been having health problems ever since I had a miscarriage June 2000. She said my health was most important thing and take care of myself and stay home as long as needed.

Have you used any assistive device, such as a cane, electric scooter, etc. for mobility?

I borrowed a walker from my doctor's office in August because I couldn't walk more than three steps at a time without having so much pain. I bought a cane, but I am planning to return it.

D.'s Story

What is your chronic illness? How long have you had this illness?

Fibromyalgia, [it was] diagnosed in April of 1997, but it was triggered by thyroid cancer in November of 1992.

Are you employed? What is your occupation?

I wish I could work. I am a writer. I do small press and e-book reviews for Romantic Times. I am working on a nonfiction book proposal for Gryphon Books and two romantic fiction novels. Some days I get more work done than others.

Have you changed your job because of your chronic illness? Have you had to quit work because of your chronic illness?

Yes, I was working as a part-time legal assistant. I went back to college as an adult and wanted to work as a research assistant, but I have not been able to do so.

Can you break your job into specific activities?

(Author's example answers, which appeared in the questionnaire, are shown in italics.)

For example, as a nonfiction writer, I brainstorm ideas for my writing project.

I do this.

I research both on-line and in primary publications, as well as with personal interviews.

I do this for my fiction and nonfiction work. I have an extensive personal library, and use the Knox County dial-up system to do local research, and the dial-up system at the University of Tennessee, Knoxville Undergraduate Library.

I organize my material, which involves the following: printing material from the files I have saved on my computer, sorting those by topic and inserting them into physical file folders, which are then filed in a filing cabinet. All of this involves a lot of movements of my hands, shoulders, and back, which can cause muscle spasms and pain as well as fatigue, which comes from sitting at a desk or computer for extended periods.

How true.

In the activities above, I pull pages from the printer, make sure they are straight, then staple them together. I type on a computer keyboard and use the mouse quite a bit.

Yes.

Besides the physical activities, my mind must be able to concentrate and focus on the material I am studying and researching. Cognitive problems can arise with a particular chronic illness or because of the medications used for treatment.

Yes, sometimes I have a terrible problem remembering words I want to use in writing and conversation.

Do you consider yourself disabled? Are you receiving any disability benefits?

I didn't used to, but I do now. The people who say this illness is not progressive should live in my shoes for a year. No, I have not had the need to apply. As long as my husband makes a good living and we have good insurance I don't plan to.

If you have changed jobs or reduced your working hours, how long ago did this happen? Has this improved your ability to work?

As long as do my work from home I am OK, relatively speaking. I can rest when I need to, and work odd hours of the day and night.

Have you taken advantage of any vocational rehabilitation training? Where did you receive this training, from a state facility or one at a university or community college or through the Social Security Administration?

No, oddly enough or not depending on your point of view, God has provided the training I needed for the computer use. I was called into a series of jobs, nonpaid, for my church where I had to learn computer basics, and then more specifics. They indirectly led to my writing and ability to make some money and feel productive. I thank God for that, or by now I would have lost my mind, and my willingness to live.

Have you told your employer about your chronic illness? What was the response? If you have not told your employer, what are your concerns about discussing your chronic illness?

If you can function and not have to tell your employer, more power to you. However, I don't know many fibromyalgia patients who can do this. Most employers run out of sympathy when you don't show signs of improving, even after following the doctors' advice.

Have you used any assistive device, such as a cane, electric scooter, etc. for mobility? Have you used anything to make doing your job any easier, such as an ergonomic computer keyboard, ergonomically designed office chair, voice recognition software? If so, what and how well did it work?

Right now the only thing I use is a cane, and as the stress increases in my life so does the need to use it. We are going through a very stressful time, as we are moving my in-laws out of the house where they have lived for more than thirty years. There is one sibling who is making it harder than it has to be. My sister is moving; she has lived behind me for more than ten years and I depend on her a lot. My in-laws are moving into where my sister now lives; so we will be their primary caregivers, and my youngest is leaving home for college in three weeks. My daughter-in-law is very ill, and has been since the 4th of July, and they still can't find out what is wrong with her. It will get easier once we get everyone moved, but right now it is a great deal of stress.

S.'s Story

What is your chronic illness?

Chronic depression, arthritis, the onset of fibromyalgia.

How long have you had to this illness?

[It was] thirteen years [ago] when it became a real problem.

Are you employed? What is your occupation?

No, I'm on disability.

Have you changed your job because of your chronic illness?

Yes, several times.

Have you had to quit work because of your chronic illness?

Yes.

Can you break your job into specific activities?

My work is the same as Gayle's, except that I'm a fiction writer. Just being able to type, click on the mouse, manipulate the papers and stapler, the paper clips, and using the concentration needed to plot a book, research, talk with other writers online is more than I can do on some days. It causes spasms and pain, which breaks the concentration.

And as Gayle has mentioned, the medications do interfere. I try to reduce my medication when trying to work, and this sometimes causes more pain.

Do you consider yourself disabled?

I try not to. That's a negative attitude, but I had to face my limitations.

Are you receiving any disability benefits?
Yes, I receive SSI.

If you have changed jobs or reduced your working hours, how long ago did this happen?
I quit working in 1993 outside of the home.

Have you taken advantage of any vocational rehabilitation training?
Yes.

Where did you receive this training, from a state facility or one at a university or community college or through the Social Security Administration?
I took two home courses with Writer's Digest.

Have you told your employer about your chronic illness?
When I was working, I did tell them.

What was the response?
They were very supportive as they'd seen me suffer trying to do my job.

If you have not told your employer, what are your concerns about discussing your chronic illness?
My concerns then were they would think I was trying to find the easy way out of doing my work. I was afraid that if I had to apply for disability, they wouldn't be supportive. Also, I didn't want to let them down.

Have you used any assistive device, such as a cane, electric scooter, etc. for mobility?
Yes, a cane, for a short time.

Have you used anything to make doing your job any easier, such as an ergonomic computer keyboard, ergonomically designed office chair, voice recognition software? If so, what and how well did it work?
I use a high-back executive chair to support my back and shoulders better, a cordless mouse that I position on the keyboard shelf of my desk to limit my range of motion in my shoulder. I put my keyboard in my lap. When I have to be in bed or in a different, more comfort-

able space, I use a laptop. The ergonomic keyboards are uncomfortable for me.

Voice recognition software at this point would make me feel less capable than I already feel. I'm glad it's available though. I have to limit my time at my desk, too. Also, I put soothing music on my CD. It seems to relax me more, and my concentration is better. I am trying meditation, too.

D.'s Story

What is your chronic illness?
Mine began in June of 2000 with viral meningitis. After having a seizure, I then became ill with CFS (chronic fatigue syndrome).

How long have you had this illness?
About fourteen months now.

Are you employed? What is your occupation?
I am an office manager in a law office. I have worked there for thirteen years. I also used to be a producer in a community theater but had to stop doing that due to lack of strength.

Have you changed your job because of your chronic illness?
My job in the law office is now part-time, and I hired a friend (who has fibromyalgia and is on disability) to help me with some of the work.

Have you had to quit work because of your chronic illness?
I was out of work for three months, but then returned part-time. However, some days are very difficult.

Can you break your job into specific activities?
I work on different types of legal cases and can separate some activities. I try and do some of my phone calls to clients or insurance adjusters from home. I also do some computer work at home; for example, I can type some legal briefs, interrogatories and documents like that at home, and that way can rest if I get tired. Some work must be kept in the office as I can't carry the files home with me and need information that is in the files.

Do you consider yourself disabled?
I do, but I don't think my doctor does, which presents a problem for me. That is why I continue to try and work, as it is my only source of income.

Are you receiving any disability benefits?

No.

If you have changed jobs or reduced your working hours, how long ago did this happen?

As I mentioned, I used to work an eight-hour day, five days a week. Now I work a three- to five-hour day, six to seven days a week.

Has this improved your ability to work?

It has helped, but it leaves me no time for anything else in my life but resting and working.

Have you taken advantage of any vocational rehabilitation training?

No, this was not necessary.

Have you told your employer about your chronic illness?

Yes, I have.

What was the response?

He has been very sympathetic, and even sometimes will drive me to work. If I don't feel well during the day, he will take me home early (which has happened many times). I thought honesty was the best policy. I didn't want the stress of trying to pretend that everything was OK.

Have you used any assistive device, such as a cane, electric scooter, etc. for mobility?

Not at the present time. During my first two months of the illness, if I went to the doctor I used a wheelchair.

Have you used anything to make doing your job any easier, such as an ergonomic computer keyboard, ergonomically designed office chair, voice recognition software? If so, what and how well did it work?

I have not tried any of these things.

B.'s Story

What is your chronic illness? How long have you had this illness?

I have osteoarthritis in my knees. The doctor told me I had the knees of a seventy-year-old, several years ago. They have been bone-on-bone for several years. I have a fusion of my lower spine, the bottom three vertebrae. The arthritis has spread to my hands, toes, ankles and has really spread in my spine. There is pressure on the sciatic nerves down the left and right side. Whenever there is a twinge or an ache in any other joint it really scares me.

I have had this since about 1989. It all started right after I was in an explosion at the chemical plant where I worked. Oh, by the way, I am fifty—will be fifty-one on 9/2/01.

I worked a "man's job" for twenty-four years. I have been off work this last time since April 2000. I was off six months in 1993, when I had back surgery. Then I had surgery in 1997 on my leg—to straighten the alignment of my leg and buy me some more time before a replacement. There was a problem with it healing and I was off for the whole year.

Are you employed? What is your occupation?

Not employed. I was an operator in a chemical plant for twenty-two years and for two years before that I worked in a carbon black plant. At present, I am on long-term disability.

Have you changed your job because of your chronic illness?

I was never able to change jobs because of my illness. That was not an option at the place I worked and the type of job I had. With the back problems, the walking was not the only problem; I cannot sit for very long at a time.

Have you had to quit work because of your chronic illness?

Yes. I stayed as long as I was able. When I went back in 1998, the doctor tried to discourage it, but I felt like I had no choice because I was my sole support and source of insurance. Of course, things just got worse and worse no matter how much I tried to save myself.

Can you break your job into specific activities?

At my job I had to do a lot of climbing, stairs and ladders. A lot of walking, opening and closing big valves, standing, and every three days—sitting at a computer for twelve hours. Some lifting and a lot of trouble-shooting process problems. Not only physically, but mentally and emotionally it was very stressful, so that made it all worse. The stress caused tension in my muscles and that, in turn, really aggravated the sciatica.

Do you consider yourself disabled? Are you receiving any disability benefits?

Yes, I consider myself disabled. I am currently receiving long-term disability insurance and Social Security Disability.

If you have changed jobs or reduced your working hours, how long ago did this happen? Has this improved your ability to work?

I stopped working in April 2000. I thought that by not abusing myself any longer and getting rid of a lot of the stress, that maybe it would slow the progress of the disease. It did not, and the doctor said he didn't think it would. The only thing better is I can get my rest and do not have to risk hurting myself really bad by falling or any of the things I was required to do. Also, I have time to get the kind of exercise that the doctor recommends—bicycle and swimming pool.

Have you taken advantage of any vocational rehabilitation training?

No.

Have you told your employer about your chronic illness?

Yes, they were aware of the problems and that they were related to the explosion.

What was the response?

It was all ignored. The incident was treated like it never happened.

Have you used any assistive device, such as a cane, electric scooter, etc. for mobility?

I occasionally use a cane. I have an electric scooter for going places where there will be a lot of walking and limited places to sit. I really do not want to have to always be stuck at home and miss out on life. I also have one of those walkers on wheels that has a seat. I take it when I go shopping if there is someone to help by pushing the basket. If not, I can usually get by leaning on the basket as long as I don't take too long.

S.'s Story

What is your chronic illness?

Osteoarthritis in major joints and severe hearing loss.

How long have you had this illness?
Osteoarthritis—five years, hearing loss—twenty-one years.

Are you employed? What is your occupation?
No.

Have you had to quit work because of your chronic illness?
Yes, after thirty-two years of factory work I had to quit. I was in danger of being fired.

Can you break your job into specific activities?
I was a machine operator in the plastics manufacturing industry. My last job, I was there eleven years. I ran plastic molding machines, which also required trimming of parts, then packaging parts. The company makes lab equipment. My job required speed and accuracy. I also had to stack finished goods and did a lot of reaching and being on my feet for eight hours just got to be too much. I got to the point that I could not carry out my duties in a timely manner. I also became ill quite often, so I was threatened in a letter from human resources. I felt I had to leave.

Do you consider yourself disabled?
Yes.

Are you receiving any disability benefits?
Yes, Social Security Disability.

Have you taken advantage of any vocational rehabilitation training?
Yes, I did.

Where did you receive this training, from a state facility or one at a university or community college or through the Social Security Administration?
Vesid-vocational Educational Rehabilitation Department through the State of New York.

Have you told your employer about your chronic illness?
Yes.

What was the response?
You should think about leaving and try for SSD.

Have you used any assistive device, such as a cane, electric scooter, etc. for mobility?

Cane.

Have you used anything to make doing your job any easier, such as an ergonomic computer keyboard, ergonomically designed office chair, voice recognition software? If so, what and how well did it work?

TTY—teletype for the deaf/VCO phone.

D.'s Story

What is your chronic illness?

Rheumatoid arthritis.

How long have you had this illness?

Since I was twenty-one. I'm forty-seven now.

Are you employed? What is your occupation?

Full-time writer.

Have you changed your job because of your chronic illness? Have you had to quit work because of your chronic illness?

I was a full-time critical care nurse until my midtwenties, in medical school to become an anesthesiologist. I did have to quit medicine at about age twenty-eight.

Can you break your job into specific activities?

As a nonfiction writer (most of the major women's magazines, nonfiction books) I research online and at universities and libraries. My typical nonfiction workday lasts about ten hours, six days a week.

As a fiction writer, my research is the same, and when I'm writing fiction, my workdays are a little less, about eight hours a day, six days a week. For nonfiction, I'm in my office at my computer at my desk that's customized to accommodate me. My desk chair is my wheelchair. For fiction I'm kicked back in my recliner with my laptop.

I teach four courses at Indiana University on how to get published; all are taught from my wheelchair.

Do you consider yourself disabled?
Absolutely. I can walk only with crutches or use a wheelchair.

Are you receiving any disability benefits?
Nope.

If you have changed jobs or reduced your working hours, how long ago did this happen?
I was a housewife/mother after I left medicine and only came to writing eight years ago when I was bored.

Has this improved your ability to work?
My career changes have been so drastic I'm not sure this applies to me.

Have you taken advantage of any vocational rehabilitation training?
Not necessary. I have graduate degrees and options other than vocational.

Have you told your employer about your chronic illness?
Not applicable. Although when I was a VA nurse, they were very good about my problems. I was still able to put in ten hours a day in intensive care, on my feet, however.

Have you used any assistive device, such as a cane, electric scooter, etc. for mobility?
Wheelchair and crutches. Also a lift chair and elevated toilet seat. My house is accessible.

Have you used anything to make doing your job any easier, such as an ergonomic computer keyboard, ergonomically designed office chair, voice recognition software? If so, what and how well did it work?
None of the above. My offices are custom-designed to fit my physical needs, though.

Author's note: When I read D.'s comment about her office being custom-designed, I asked for more information as I have some problems in getting my office to accommodate my chair.

My desk is strictly a custom design from California Closets—height, reaching distances across. It's three sides of a square, and I can roll right in, and everything's within my reach either rolling forwards or backwards. I have built-in bookshelf/storage on my lower right side (inside of the desk) and the outside that's not against the wall is one complete bookshelf (not accessible when I'm at my desk since it's on the outside). The ends are two-drawer file cabinets built in.

Also on the side to my right I have a custom bookshelf on the wall for my handy-dandy references. And I've had a custom entertainment center (accessible) for my stereo system. It was all fitted to me, my reach, my individual needs. Price close to $5,000—six years ago (counting from summer 2001). Worth every penny.

And when I kick back in my recliner, it's a lift chair. I just prop my laptop on a pillow. I also have a couple of those little travel-sized pillows for my arms since the arm rests on the chair are a bit too low. I also use a neck support. I guess the key is what's comfortable for you.

E.'s Story

What is your chronic illness?

A back injury.

How long have you had this illness?

Since December 1998.

Are you employed? What is your occupation?

I was employed. I worked in maintenance.

Have you changed your job because of your chronic illness?

I am not working at this time.

Have you had to quit work because of your chronic illness?

Yes. I could no longer meet the requirements of the job.

Can you break your job into specific activities?

Touch up paint, change lightbulbs, change batteries, repair leaky faucets/showers, replace screens, troubleshoot electrical appliances, operate a front end loader, locate frozen pipes, removal of sheet rock, fill pot holes, rebuild sprinklers, repair hot tub, use hand tools, check for gas leaks, check heating/air conditioning, clean debris, patch roof, replace windows, and rekey locks.

Do you consider yourself disabled? Are you receiving any disability benefits?

I receive permanent disability payments, but not SSD or SSI.

Have you taken advantage of any vocational rehabilitation training?

I am in retraining now.

Where did you receive this training, from a state facility or one at a university or community college or through the Social Security Administration?

I received this training through the state.

Have you used any assistive device, such as a cane, electric scooter, etc. for mobility?

I use a hot tub and a TENS unit to help with the pain.

J.'s Story

What is your chronic illness? How long have you had this illness?

I have Friedreich's ataxia. It is a hereditary, progressive neurologic condition due to the lack of the protein frataxin being produced in ganglial root and peripheral nerve cells. Frataxin's job is to eliminate iron buildup in the mitochondria; without it, iron builds up and the nerve cell sickens and dies. We began testing when I was sixteen. I was diagnosed at nineteen. I am now twenty-six.

Are you employed? What is your occupation?

I am a homemaker and a romance writer.

Have you changed your job because of your chronic illness? Have you had to quit work because of your chronic illness?

My disability limited my choices in work. I went to school, and graduated with my liberal arts degree. However, this so exhausted me that I did not continue my education. School did, however, lead me to Romance Writers of America. Writing romance has been a dream since I was little. Fatigue and the inability to drive have limited me, somewhat. I depend on others for monthly meetings and trips to the library or bookstore. I also volunteer extensively.

Can you break your job into specific activities?
I do all the things Gayle listed here. I organize, run listservs on the Internet, spend hours at the computer, and experience pain in my neck, shoulders, wrists and knees. Sitting straight up is difficult on my neck; leaning back catches the chair at my knees and raises my feet off the floor. I have gotten a laptop to ease this, but it doesn't help with the wrists.

As far as cognitive problems, fatigue is the only thing that makes this difficult. A symptom of FA is sometimes hypothyroidism, which I have. Both of these carry fatigue as a side effect.

Do you consider yourself disabled? Are you receiving any disability benefits?
Yes. I have been using a walker, and am considering moving to a scooter for longer walks. FA destroys balance, making me lurch from side to side. Even standing in one place without holding on to something is an exercise. I have no reflexes. This keeps me from driving and for the most part makes me homebound.

Have you taken advantage of any vocational rehabilitation training? Where did you receive this training, from a state facility or one at a university or community college or through the Social Security Administration?
I have. When I went to school, I was also working with Vocational Rehabilitation. When I did not continue my education past liberal arts, I was no longer working with them.

Have you used any assistive device, such as a cane, electric scooter, etc. for mobility? Have you used anything to make doing your job any easier, such as an ergonomic computer keyboard, ergonomically designed office chair, voice recognition software? If so, what and how well did it work?
Scooters at stores are a humongous help. It makes shopping so much more pleasurable to be able to sit and look at things instead of walking by in a haze of pain from my knees. As far as work, having a laptop and the ability to sit or recline in any position has worked wonders.

C.'s Story

What is your chronic illness?
Rheumatoid arthritis.

How long have you had this illness?
Twenty-six years.

Are you employed? What is your occupation?
I currently am self-employed, and am the Arthritis Guide for
About.com.

Have you changed your job because of your chronic illness?
Yes. Around 1992, when working as a registered medical technolo-
gist in a hospital lab, I reduced my schedule from full-time to part-
time due to my illness.

Have you had to quit work because of your chronic illness?
Yes. In 1993, I had to quit my job as a registered medical technolo-
gist.

Can you break your job into specific activities?
I'm responsible for producing content for the arthritis Web site on
About.com. This involves creating new content through writing,
searching the Internet for news and pertinent net links, maintaining
a community forum and chat room. My work involves answering
questions and e-mails from visitors to my site. All of the above activities involve extensive computer use.

**Do you consider yourself disabled? Are you receiving any disabil-
ity benefits?**
I don't consider myself disabled. To me that implies complete lack of
ability. I consider myself "limited." No, I am not receiving disability
benefits at this time.

**If you have changed jobs or reduced your working hours, how
long ago did this happen?**
It happened about eight or nine years ago.

Has this improved your ability to work?
It has given me the chance to work from home on my own schedule.

**Have you taken advantage of any vocational rehabilitation
training?**
No.

Have you told your employer about your chronic illness?
My employer at the hospital lab knew about my illness, as does the
staff of About.com.

What was the response?

The response was ultimately compassionate and understanding. Whenever I needed time off for surgery there was a sense of "take care of yourself, do what you need to do" and yet there was always an underlying current of "there's a job to get done here" or perhaps that was just perceived by me.

Have you used any assistive device, such as a cane, electric scooter, etc. for mobility?

Used crutches and cane only following surgeries for a limited time during rehab.

Have you used anything to make doing your job any easier, such as an ergonomic computer keyboard, ergonomically designed office chair, voice recognition software? If so, what and how well did it work?

No.

J.'s Story

What is your chronic illness?

1. Urethral syndrome. (May or may not be a form of interstitial cystitis. I've gotten conflicting diagnoses over the years.) This will flare for periods as long as a year and then goes into remission for a couple months or even sometimes years.

2. Severe ruptured discs in lower back. I was paralyzed in one side of my leg for about three weeks at first and gradually regained my muscle strength, but it took three years to become pain free most of the time, and I still have problems with any lifting, and twisting or walking more than fifteen minutes.

3. I'm borderline diabetic and have controlled my blood sugar for three years with a seriously low-carb diet.

How long have you had this illness?

1. The urinary tract problems are of fifteen years' duration.

2. The back problems started with a severe disc rupture four years ago.

3. I was discovered to have diabetic postprandial blood sugars three years ago though my fasting sugars were normal and on a low-carb diet everything looks fine (until I eat something I shouldn't!)

Are you employed? What is your occupation?

I work for my own company. I've published six nonfiction books for people in my professional field, one of which was a niche bestseller and has gone into a second edition. After my first big success with a major publisher, I published three more books through my own small press and started a Web site to promote it, which has grown into a profit center in itself, collecting and selling data of interest to people in my professional field.

By summer of 2001 I had sold 15,000 self-published books with a retail value of half a million dollars. My self-published books are in all the chains, mostly because my bestseller established me as an authority in my field.

I also recently finished a novel, which is currently with an agent.

Have you changed your job because of your chronic illness?

No. I have been working for myself for thirteen years and was home with a baby when the urinary tract problems first started.

Have you had to quit work because of your chronic illness?

No.

Can you break your job into specific activities?

I am a writer and a software developer. The activities are the same as you listed, though I find that writing code is much harder on my back than writing books (I've done eight), probably because I have to peer at the screen more intensely to debug code and I tend to hunch. Sitting for long times writing is tough on my back, and I just accept that I'm going to have some painful days after finishing up a project, but paradoxically getting wrapped up in a project takes my mind off the urinary tract problems. In fact, I've written several of my books during flares because if I am not busy every minute, having to pee starts driving me nuts.

Oddly, my back problems, unlike most people's, get much worse with walking than sitting, so even though sitting can end up causing me pain, I can live with it. What I love about my way of working is that I only work when I feel like it, so if I'm having a bad day I can crawl into bed or whatever I need to do. I work very intensely for bursts of six or seven weeks adding features to the Web site or writing a new book, and then I take months where I do little but routine maintenance on my Web site and fill orders.

I am very careful to avoid scheduling anything, ever, since I never know what kind of shape I'll be in. Sometimes I'm "normal" and other times I can barely walk or my urinary tract is in such crisis that I don't like being around people.

Do you consider yourself disabled?

No.

Are you receiving any disability benefits?

No.

If you have not told your employer, what are your concerns about discussing your chronic illness?

I maintain a high profile in my professional life since I run a very busy Web site and bulletin board for people in my field. I don't talk about my health problems (or my personal life in general) publicly as I think it detracts from the professional image I want to build, especially since professionals in my field tend to be young and male, and I feel that they'd have less confidence that I understand their issues if they saw me as a sick old lady.

The biggest limitation posed by my chronic health problems has been that I won't commit to lectures and convention appearances though I am in demand as a speaker because I never know what kind of shape I'll be in months ahead and if I'll be able to handle a public appearance. When I have a flare I may have to pee every fifteen minutes for weeks. This also makes me not schedule travel.

Have you used any assistive device, such as a cane, electric scooter, etc. for mobility?

NO. I do know where every bathroom is within 40 miles.

Have you used anything to make doing your job any easier, such as an ergonomic computer keyboard, ergonomically designed office chair, voice recognition software? If so, what and how well did it work?

I have an ergo keyboard which eliminated all carpal tunnel symptoms some years ago. I have a seriously "UNergo" work setup, but I have a tiny space for my office and keep thinking we'll move, and I'll be able to set up a fancy one. Still, I've been so successful with my writing using this uncomfortable setup I'm loathe to mess with anything.

Additional comments

I found the *Living with Chronic Illness* book by Cheri Register very helpful when I first started having problems. The important thing to get across is that most books about chronic disease are much too negative. The books about IC [interstitial cystitis] told me I could expect to lose my husband and perhaps become suicidal. This wasn't what I needed to hear after diagnosis when I was in intense pain and miserable!

In fact, I did lose my husband, who, among other things, couldn't handle what he called my "ailments." But several years later I met a wonderful man, much younger than I am, who has stuck with me through almost six years including the paralyzing back injury and several long IC flares. We have the kind of sex life that got me writing romance novels. And this started when I was menopausal, "wrinkley," and nine years out from my IC diagnosis!

I never dreamed I'd find a handsome, brilliant, loving man who would adore me with all my health problems just because of who I am. I suspect that the inner strength and creativity I've had to develop by not being able to live a "normal" life has given me a lot more personality than I had when I was young. And I've learned that though sometimes I'm not functional, other times I'm fine and my sweetie is willing to wait for those times because we are so happy together then.

So I wish I'd known how much happiness I could have in life despite the health problems back when they first developed in my late thirties and felt like I'd gotten a death sentence from my doctor.

Also, I have three serious conditions which aren't well understood and have pretty much had to teach myself medicine at home in my spare time to deal with them. I've come up with some treatments for my urinary tract problems that have been very helpful through reading, Internet searching, and experimentation. My alternative diabetes diet, though still quite controversial, has kept my blood sugar completely normal for three years and impresses my doctor now. At this point I go to the doctor and tell him what I need him to prescribe and he usually does, as he knows I've done my research.

But it is frustrating how little interest most doctors have in helping you with chronic conditions that aren't fatal. Being in pain seems to be a "so what" to doctors when the test results are iffy.

I got to where I was actually thrilled when I had blood in my urine because for several years they'd been sending me away as a crank when I'd show up with intense frequency and pain and it was only when I had blood or white cells in the urine that they went from treating me as a crank to treating me as a patient. Similarly, I was treated like a crank with the back problems until the MRI showed a huge mass extruded from a disc crunching a nerve, but I had to fight like hell to get the MRI. It shouldn't be like that!

That reminds me of one last anecdote that might be useful to you. Years ago, when I had my first long urinary tract flare I went to a gynecologist thinking that the problem might be related to injuries suffered at my son's birth. The doctor, an older man, informed me that my problems were psychological. Obviously, he said, I was consumed by a fear of failure and was using disease to hide from this fear of failure at work.

I let him finish and then explained that far from that being the case, I'd just sold a professional book to a major publisher and was looking forward to a book tour. "Oh," sez the doc without dropping a stitch, "Then it's clear your psychological problem is that you are afraid of success!"

There are too many doctors like this and their advice is toxic. Find something you love and do it when you can. I was very lucky that I didn't have to support myself for a couple years and could build up the business over time (I got child support and some help from my parents when I started it, but now make a serious income from my business). I didn't plan it, one thing just led to another, but everything was something I loved and found interesting, and eventually, it all fell together for me.

K.'s Story

What is your chronic illness?

Neuropathy, inherited tendency to pressure palsy.

How long have you had this illness?

Diagnosed in July 2001. On February 4, 2001, I fell on my butt and ruptured a disc at C4–C5. Surgery had to be done on April 9, 2001, due to the severity of the rupture—it was very close to severing the spinal cord.

I'm now experiencing arm and leg pain. The EMG shows no

nerve response at the ankles or wrists. The neurologist at first suggested that it may be neuropathy, but now says it may be Inherited Tendency to Pressure Palsy. This is a condition that is inherited from a parent and to the best of his knowledge, has no treatment.

Are you employed? What is your occupation?

Employed at **** Insurance as an insurance specialist.

Have you changed your job because of your chronic illness?

Not yet.

Have you had to quit work because of your chronic illness?

Am on short-term disability at this time.

Can you break your job into specific activities?

I work in a call center environment. My primary responsibility is to assist members with current policies and to issue new policies for auto, home, personal articles, condos, and rental properties. My workday is $9^{1}/_{2}$ hours and $8^{1}/_{2}$ of those hours I need to be logged on the phone ready to assist members. I also assist other employees to find information and to do referrals for complex policy issues or increases. The time on the computer is difficult.

I find the pain increases even with frequent breaks. At home, I am able to lie down and take my pain meds—this is not a reality in the work environment. Underwriting is involved with new issues and many times it is solely up to me to issue a policy or not based on the information I have obtained. When I am hurting, it is very difficult to concentrate on the call. A simple matter of someone telling me that a front porch needs repair can be reason for decline (depending on the damage). Though this may sound insignificant, a porch in disrepair can be a liability exposure for the member and the insurance company. It is up to me to discover this information and advise the member of the appropriate actions.

Do you consider yourself disabled?

I refuse to consider myself disabled. I am physically challenged (some say mentally—grin!).

Are you receiving any disability benefits?

Short-term disability from my employer.

Have you taken advantage of any vocational rehabilitation training?

No.

Have you told your employer about your chronic illness?

Employer is informed of diagnosis.

What was the response?

None at this time.

Have you used any assistive device, such as a cane, electric scooter, etc. for mobility?

No.

Have you used anything to make doing your job any easier, such as an ergonomic computer keyboard, ergonomically designed office chair, voice recognition software? If so, what and how well did it work?

Have had ergonomic keyboard for $3\frac{1}{2}$ years.

N.'s Story

What is your chronic illness? How long have you had this illness?

I have CFS (chronic fatigue syndrome), FMS (fibromyalgia syndrome), MPS (myofascial pain syndrome), and arthritis. I've had CFS for seventeen years and FMS, MPS & arthritis for thirteen years.

Are you employed? What is your occupation?

I am retired. But I have been taking care of my grandson three or four days a week while his mother and father work. I am able to do general housework and perhaps a little yard work. But I have to pace myself carefully. If I have a lot of errands to do, I generally must not do any strenuous work such as vacuuming. If I have a lot of mental work to do, that same day I really have to limit physical activity. It's important to take frequent rest breaks. I am able to drive, but I stay off of busy interstates.

Have you had to quit work because of your chronic illness?

I took early retirement because of my illness.

Do you consider yourself disabled? Are you receiving any disability benefits?

Yes, but I retired rather than apply for disability as my employer said there was no such thing as chronic fatigue syndrome. Another coworker tried and failed.

If you have changed jobs or reduced your working hours, how long ago did this happen? Has this improved your ability to work?

I tried to work part-time after retiring, but learning a new position with the cognitive problems I had with CFS was impossible.

Have you taken advantage of any vocational rehabilitation training?

There was nothing available.

Have you told your employer about your chronic illness?

I did before I retired because of my high absences toward the end.

What was the response?

I was told there was no such thing as CFS and that it was purely psychological. I would advise people NOT to do that, but to focus on particular symptoms such as pain. However, neurological testing is available to prove cognitive disability at this time.

Additional comments

1. Find treatment for all symptoms if possible. Long distance travel to a specialist is preferable so that you try all treatment alternatives before giving up and have to accept a lower-level position or ultimately applying for disability.

    a. Menopause can exacerbate any symptom and is treatable with natural estrogen that will diminish or eliminate undesirable symptoms that greatly aggravate a chronic condition.

    b. CFS/FMS can usually affect cognitive ability. There is treatment to slow down that process for some people.

    c. Neurological testing will identify any cognitive impairment that will aid in getting placed into a more appropriate position. Get legal representation to know your rights for getting cooperation from your employer.

    d. Nutrition education will identify any weak areas or deficiencies. Fatigue is increased by inadequate diet. For example, most doctors will not test for mineral deficiency. I was found to have a severe deficiency in magnesium and calcium and am now supplementing them.

2. Never tell your employer that you have CFS or FMS as there is still far too much ignorance about these disorders and they are assumed to be purely psychological. *(See note below.)* Get help from various specialists such as a neurologist for chronic pain or disabling neurological symptoms like dizziness, balance problems, etc. Get help from a pain specialist for fibromyalgia. Not all cities have pain specialists who understand FMS. It may be necessary to travel to another city to get appropriate treatment. There are CFS/FMS specialists who are helpful in providing treatment and working with a patient's primary care doctor and facilitate being able to continue working.

3. Be sure that pain is identified as what it is. For example, some forms of arthritis are not visible on an x-ray. An MRI may be necessary.

4. Not all rheumatologists understand the complexities of FMS and often confuse it with chronic fatigue syndrome and thereby assume it is psychological. *(See note below.)*

5. Seek help from a counselor/therapist that deals with patients living with chronic illness and are knowledgeable of these particular disorders.

6. If possible, take a six-month leave of absence from your job to determine if this is a permanent or temporary disorder. Also use this time to research your illness and treatment. It's virtually impossible to do this and hold down a full-time job for severely ill patients.

Probably one of the most important things a person who is trying to hang on to their job and is dealing with cognitive difficulties can do is to find a psychologist who does neuro-cognitive testing. Fortunately, patients with CFS/FMS in the Charlotte area have a good one in Dr. Jeffrey Ewert. This test measures all cognitive deficits, which conclusively evaluates the ability of the patient in making decisions about possible job changing.

Author's note: While this does happen, I have generally found that more and more doctors, from family practitioners to rheumatologists, are becoming more aware of both of the conditions. It is certainly more difficult for those individuals with conditions like these where there is no one definitive lab test that can provide the diagnosis. Because the cause of many of these conditions such as CFS or FM is unknown, the treatment most often is directed toward relief of the symptoms and is not always effective. These are part of the "invisible disabilities."

P.'s Story

What is your chronic illness?

Migraines, allergies, sinus stuff, depression, and neck/shoulder/back pain.

How long have you had this illness?

Migraines since age thirteen (I'm now thirty-nine); allergies and sinus for maybe eight years (don't really remember when it started); depression for almost seven years (following complete hysterectomy—I think it screwed my chemical balance); neck/shoulder pain started three–four years ago when a metal end cap sign holder fell on my head while I was squatting over books I was putting on an end cap. Being rear-ended in a car accident a year ago reactivated the problems with neck and shoulder pain. Often my back will hurt, too. [When I'm] reaching up high to shelve books, straighten[ing up] really hurts within a few minutes. Hoisting boxes, too.

Are you employed?

Yes.

What is your occupation?

Full-time supervisor at [a bookstore].

Have you changed your job because of your chronic illness?

For the most part, there isn't much I can change about where I work, though I did put a screen on one of the computers because it drove me crazy every time I walked by it—felt like it was going to trigger a migraine. Flickering flourescent lights will also trigger a migraine. Also perfumes, lotions, etc. Bright sunlight, too.

Books attract dust, which aggravates my sinus and allergy stuff. If I'm in the middle of a bout of depression and the meds aren't really doing their job, then difficult customers, boss, coworkers, etc. can exacerbate it.

Have you had to quit work because of your chronic illness?

No, but I would like to quit; not an option because, though I don't make enough to live on, it does help pay the rent and buy groceries, and we have our insurance through my job.

Can you break your job into specific activities?

Sure, but boy, are you going to be sorry you asked!

Customer service: Greeting customers, answering the phone; finding books for customers; taking customer to the section and putting the book in their hands; ordering books for customers; tracking down orders that never arrive; ringing up books at the cashwrap; offering the [discount card] to each and every customer; offering additional merchandise; telling each customer about our [returns] policy. Shortlist all books customers request, but we don't have, or are out of, as well as books we're low on.

Receiving: Open back door for shipments; record the shipper, # of boxes, and the time on the receiving log; separating the boxes into customer orders, frontlist, backlist, re-stock order, bargain, and gift. Scanning each box (or each book in some of the boxes). Matching up customer order slips with their respective books and take the books up to the cashwrap so the storefront cashier can call the customers. Putting some of the frontlist books on a v-cart for the storefront cashier to put away. Put the rest of the frontlist and the backlist titles on one of four H-carts, which are separated into "zones." The books are placed on the cart to correspond with each zone's layout with the category sheet in front of each category of book. Each category is also alphabetized. Boxes of bargain books are taken up front for the storefront cashier to put away. Some of the bargain books require printing stickers and applying the stickers before taking them up front. All boxes are to be received and on the sales floor within twenty-four hours. Sweep floor, take out trash, and clean off receiving table.

Merchandising: Set up new displays (CGWs, promo plexi, endcaps, Books Today wall, new fiction table, new nonfiction table) every month according to the corporate instructions, which arrive toward the end of the month (also means the original display must be taken down and the books shelved).

There are also optional displays that need to be refreshened or changed. Several times a year (Christmas, Easter, Mother's Day, Father's Day, clearance sales) the front bargain table is converted to its special purpose, which involves moving lots of books to different bargain barges. Last Christmas I changed out at least four bargain barges, which hold at least fifty titles (less if large, coffee-table size books).

Zone maintenance: Go through every section of every zone and scan each title to make sure it's in the correct section and in the proper order. If it's due out on return to the publisher, the book is pulled and labeled by vendor. Return books are then taken to back room and sorted on the return shelves, which have vendor labels. Strip returns are stripped and the covers filed.

Returns: Scan (and desticker), pack, retrieve return document from computer on sales floor, weigh, label, and ship books to their respective vendors. Stripped covers are scanned, rubber banded by vendor, and packed, return doc placed inside, labeled, and shipped. Some returns are "consolidated," which means they go by truck and we have to fill out a bill of lading, recording each box along with its weight and return doc number. Returns to smaller vendors are shipped out UPS, which requires inputting shipping info into the UPS machine and attaching the UPS labels and bar codes to the boxes.

Supervisory functions: Bookseller assignments, double-check that assignments are being done and are being done correctly, handle returns/exchanges/institutional sales/complaints/requests for donations, print/read/file email and corporate pc messages plus reply or take appropriate action, count down register drawers, opening and closing procedures on the manager's terminal, Sunday—do payroll, daily sales recap, record information into sales notebook, prepare deposit, take deposit to bank, enter deposit into register, put deposit slip into daily media envelope. Once a week, daily and weekly media envelopes shipped to corporate office.

Magazines: Arrive several times a week. Are to be on newsstand before the end of the day. Old issues are taken off, stripped, and filed for return.

Recovery: Going through store, straightening, putting away books left lying around by customers.

Tuesdays: New PLU list arrives, telling us which books are on the bestseller fixtures. These must be stickered/destickered. The bestseller fixtures must be changed to correspond with the new lists. Books we are low on must be shortlisted so more can be ordered.

Inventory is reviewed and ordered daily. Keep up with new releases by reading the book catalogs. I also hold books for quite a few customers (research the book catalogs and tag them in the computer for customers).

Clearance sales (twice a year? I forget) and bargain markdowns require taking the pull lists sent to us and pulling the items from the sales floor, stickering them, and displaying them.

Throw in periodic visits from the district manager and occasionally the regional manager, customer shops where we're graded by people we don't know are grading us, inventory, Christmas season, store meetings, and occasional book signings and book fairs.

Also, sales floor must be dust mopped (wood floor) or vacuumed (carpet). Lightbulbs replaced. Fixtures dusted. Plexi windexed. Cashwrap cleaned, dusted, and windexed.

This is probably way more information than you were looking for and I'm sure I've forgotten something. It's a very physical job because those boxes are heavy. Lot of bending and squatting involved when shelving, zone maintenance, helping customers. On your feet. Lot of reaching, which really makes my neck and shoulders hurt. Climbing ladders to put away or retrieve books.

Also draining on the brain because most customers don't know what they are looking for (blue book; on Oprah; has a nine-year-old nephew, but doesn't have a clue what the kid is interested in; author's last name is Minniger, they think, but don't know for sure or how to spell it; no, they don't want to order it, they need it today and are we sure we don't have it in the back room?) Lots of math involved (change to customers; recaps; deposits; change orders; amount saved with readers advantage card; formulas to figure workload and schedule; profit and loss stuff, etc.).

Computer and mouse involved to look up books, place customer orders, inventory management, open and close store, update customer orders, clock in and out, shortlist titles, etc. Computers also used for cashiering, without a mouse. Adding machine used for counting drawers, daily recap, deposit, sales figures, etc. PDTs (personal data transmitter) are hand-held and used by everyone doing zone maintenance, receiving books, and returning books.

Do you consider yourself disabled?

No, not really because I'm not in a wheelchair and I don't require a cane or other assistance walking.

If you have changed jobs or reduced your working hours, how long ago did this happen?

I can't afford to. If headache is too bad, I'll use sick time, but even that is limited.

Has this improved your ability to work?

It probably would if I could do it.

Have you taken advantage of any vocational rehabilitation training?

No.

Have you told your employer about your chronic illness?

Yep.

What was the response?

She sent me to the hospital for work comp; allows me to use sick time when needed, if we have enough coverage.

If you have not told your employer, what are your concerns about discussing your chronic illness?

I know she gets tired of hearing about it, because it seems like I never feel good, or at least not for long. Can't remember the last time I went through a day without my head or my shoulders or neck (sometimes all at once) bothering me.

Have you used any assistive device, such as a cane, electric scooter, etc. for mobility?

No.

S.'s Story (UK)

What is your chronic illness?

Chronic fatigue syndrome.

How long have you had this illness?

Seriously for three years with at least an eighteen-month lead-in, getting more and more tired and coping less and less well. I also have mild repetitive strain injury (RSI).

Are you employed? What is your occupation?

Not now. I worked for myself before, doing some computer consultancy and also doing complementary therapy (aromatherapy, counseling).

Have you changed your job because of your chronic illness?

I certainly gave both those up when I became sufficiently tired to pose a competency risk—but I had already given up the aromatherapy as it was doing massage that gave me RSI! Nor can I go back to them as both are stressful and stress gives me minor relapses now and major stress is a known indicator for major relapses.

So now I am trying to write. But I cannot say I am succeeding very well, as too many things still drain my energy. I am still registered by my doctor as unable to work.

Have you had to quit work because of your chronic illness?

Yes, two and a half years ago.

Can you break your job into specific activities?

This is a bit hard, as I don't think I could class what I do as writing yet. I read for research—but find I cannot concentrate on nonfiction for more than half an hour or so. I download, read, and answer my e-mails. This can be tiring and I find that these days I am not sufficiently discriminating to filter out the uninteresting, which uses up more of my precious energy and concentration.

But when I get down to the nitty-gritty of writing—I can come up with outline plots but get very bogged down with details. I can develop characters okay. But at present, the concentration needed to sit down day by day and write is beyond me. Some days I can manage and others I can do little but curl up and read.

Do you consider yourself disabled?

No, just not well.

Are you receiving any disability benefits?

No, but only because my national insurance contributions were not sufficient.

If you have changed jobs or reduced your working hours, how long ago did this happen? Has this improved your ability to work?

For the first year of my illness, I made no attempt to do anything much, as I had so little concentration. Then I started to do some research and to do some short on-line courses to improve my writing skill.

Have you told your employer about your chronic illness? What was the response? If you have not told your employer, what are your concerns about discussing your chronic illness?

As I employed myself, I could avoid it! My response was to close my little company down.

Have you used any assistive device, such as a cane, electric scooter, etc. for mobility?

A cane in the early days.

Have you used anything to make doing your job any easier, such as an ergonomic computer keyboard, ergonomically designed office chair, voice recognition software? If so, what and how well did it work?

I got an ergonomic keyboard & chair when I first got signs of RSI—my mouse mat also has a wrist support. I find it hard to type with my wrists actually supported, though. I now use voice recognition software—I tried last year, but didn't have a powerful enough computer for it to be effective. Since purchasing a 1Ghz at Xmas, I have found it much easier, although I had to invest a great deal of time training it (I have a soft voice). If my wrists begin to ache at all, I have splints to limit movement, which really help.

Additional comments

Sorry, perhaps this isn't terribly helpful. What I find most frustrating is "the spirit is willing but the flesh is weak." I desperately *want* to get down to writing, but I just don't seem to be able to get there. My teenage son says the worst thing about me being ill is that I get "ratty" a lot—having previously been pretty laid back. That "rattiness" is almost always the result of being frustrated that I cannot accomplish what I want to get done. If I stop and let go, my energy eventually comes back up.

CFS is like snakes and ladders—when you start out, you have lots of long snakes and short ladders, but as you slowly get better, the ladders get longer and the snakes shorter—except just before the end when there are several snakes which take you all the way back to the bottom. It is a disease which requires surrender, rather than something like cancer, which responds to fight.

G.'s Story

What is your chronic illness?

RSD (reflex sympathetic dystrophy, a neurological pain condition), cervical and lumbar fusion.

How long have you had this illness?

Since 1995.

Are you employed? What is your occupation?

No; nurse.

Have you changed your job because of your chronic illness? Have you had to quit work because of your chronic illness?

Yes.

Do you consider yourself disabled?

Yes, I do consider myself disabled. I did apply for Social Security but got denied. Appealed it and am waiting for reply.

Have you taken advantage of any vocational rehabilitation training?

No.

Have you told your employer about your chronic illness?

They were aware of it.

What was the response?

They made a light-duty position for me.

Have you used any assistive device, such as a cane, electric scooter, etc. for mobility?

Occasionally a walking stick.

S.'s Story

What is your chronic illness?

Desert Storm syndrome, fibromyalgia.

How long have you had this illness?
Since 1991.

Are you employed?
No.

What is your occupation?
My previous occupations with this illness were C5 loadmaster, neonatal intensive care nurse, vacation sales representative.

Have you changed your job because of your chronic illness?
Yes.

Have you had to quit work because of your chronic illness?
Yes.

Do you consider yourself disabled?
Yes!, Yes!, Yes!

Are you receiving any disability benefits?
I have applied for them from the Veterans Administration and Social Security.

If you have changed jobs or reduced your working hours, how long ago did this happen?
I went from being a neonatal intensive care nurse working alternating day and night shifts, to a human resource department job working days, Monday through Friday, to working part time in a vacation reservations office inbound calls.

Has this improved your ability to work?
NO!

Have you taken advantage of any vocational rehabilitation training?
Haven't been offered it yet, but I will try truck driving. There is no other job I can think of that I would be able to work at because of my anxiety levels dealing with other people.

Where did you receive this training, from a state facility or one at a university or community college or through the Social Security Administration?
SS or VA.

Have you told your employer about your chronic illness? What was the response?

The Air Force knew from 1994 to 2001, and did not even try to adjust my working hours, nor give me a medical discharge even though I was missing 20–30 days of work a year, had severe medicine reactions, exercise intolerance, obesity, emotional problems dealing with my coworkers and bosses, depression, pain, etc. I had to quit my part-time reservations telephone job because I was still so stressed out and depressed from the last eight years. They knew about my illness, but did not make any accommodations for it, although there was really nothing they could have done.

If you have not told your employer, what are your concerns about discussing your chronic illness?

Even though I am not working now, in my experience there are two reactions that you get when you tell your employer. One, they can not see anything wrong with you, so any complaints, problems dealing with work, or repeated work absences are looked at as a worker problem, not as a result of illness. The other is that they view you as an ill person and therefore don't want to have anything to do with you to avoid the hassle.

Have you used any assistive device, such as a cane, electric scooter, etc. for mobility?

Not yet.

Have you used anything to make doing your job any easier, such as an ergonomic computer keyboard, ergonomically designed office chair, voice recognition software? If so, what and how well did it work?

I am still learning about how my body reacts to my disease even after eleven years. I am still learning the cause and effects. I was having severe wrist pain at the reservations job from using the mouse all day. I got a tap pad, with my own money, and that helped with the wrist pain, but then I started to develop finger pain. I tried to find a chair that was comfortable and supported my back, but I still got neck and shoulder pain from repetitive movement, and I got a stiff back from sitting so long. The thing is that you are always trading off one problem for another with fibromyalgia because you have a neuroendocrine disorder! Until you fix that, NOTHING is going to be better. As a nurse I have had bushels of ergonomic training to do muscular tasks correctly.

Sure, I don't get muscle strains, sprains, etc., but I still have the underlying disorder that causes muscular pain with ANY repetitive movement. That will never go away with any kind of training. It must be cured.

T.'s Story

What is your chronic illness? How long have you had it?

I've had fibromyalgia, myofascial pain syndrome, chronic fatigue for thirteen years, also bulging disc & DDD (degenerative disc disease).

Are you employed? What is your occupation?

No, am filing for SSDI.

Have you changed your job because of your occupation? Have you had to quit work because of your chronic illness?

Had changed from oilfield in 1988 to counter person at parts store. Yes.

Do you consider yourself disabled? Are you receiving any disability benefits?

Yes. No.

Have you taken advantage of any vocational rehabilitation training?

NO.

Have you told your employer about your chronic illness? What was the response?

When I was working, it didn't matter to my employer, until I started missing so much work.

Have you used any assistive device, such as a cane, electric scooter, etc. for mobility?

Yes, I walk with a cane since I fell through a canvas chair and fell to cement hard. That's where they discovered through an MRI that I have a bulging disc, and degenerative disc disease.

S.'s Story

What is your chronic illness? How long have you had this illness?
FM for about fifteen years.

Are you employed? What is your occupation?
I was manager of a sub store.

Have you changed your job because of your chronic illness?
Yes.

Have you had to quit work because of your chronic illness?
Yes.

Can you break your job into specific activities?
I did payroll, managed seven to ten employees, ordered and accepted deliveries, did weekly inventory and sent to headquarters, made subs, party subs, used an advanced computer register, opened and closed store.

Do you consider yourself disabled?
Sometimes more than others.

Are you receiving any disability benefits?
No.

If you have changed jobs or reduced your working hours, how long ago did this happen?
I lost my job 6/01.

Has this improved your ability to work?
Well, I have been able to rest and reduce my stress level.

Have you taken advantage of any vocational rehabilitation training?
Not this time, but I have before.

Where did you receive this training, from a state facility or one at a university or community college or through the Social Security Administration?
Vocational school twice.

Have you told your employer about your chronic illness?
Yes.

What was the response?
Oh, well!

Have you used any assistive device, such as a cane, electric scooter, etc. for mobility?
No.

Have you used anything to make doing your job any easier, such as an ergonomic computer keyboard, ergonomically designed office chair, voice recognition software? If so, what and how well did it work?
No.

Index

241